The Peace of Heaven

a treasury of faith, hope and love

DANA HOWARD

Dedication

I dedicate this book to Robyn Ahearn, who encouraged me to write over the years. Many of the words of encouragement in this book were God's heart poured out through my hand when she needed a word of faith, hope, love, and peace.

Preface

This treasury of faith, hope and love was birthed out of adversity. It came through years of enduring trials that nearly cost me my life. Out of the ashes came this book written for those who could use words of hope, love, and encouragement to walk into a future filled with blessings that come from God. His peace is awaiting you as you come to spend time in His presence.

There are so many lost and broken hearts in this world and I believe that all of us, from one time to another need that voice of encouragement to help us make it through our days which can often times be filled with trials and tribulations. *The Peace of Heaven* is a book that I believe will fill you with hope and encouragement and help you embrace the great and amazing love of God inspiring you to draw closer to the Him through your daily walk of life.

I have personally been through some great trials in my life and it was out of my desperation to find hope and a path to personal freedom that I developed a relationship with Jesus Christ that gave me the hope to keep pressing forward despite the odds. Without God, I don't know if I could have made it through. He was the strength I needed to walk through the fire yet come out on the other side victoriously.

I spent many years struggling with deep depression with a diagnosis of Bipolar Disorder. I was not able to cope with some of the life events that were taking place so I would just pull the covers over my head and sleep all day for days on end. It was difficult to just do the normal activities of daily life. Despite it all, I kept looking up to God and He would give me the hope I needed to make it through my days.

I would like to share how I started on this journey that led to writing *The Peace of Heaven*. Years ago, when I was at a Christian women's retreat, the speaker asked us to take out a piece of paper and write on the top, "Dear Daughter". He asked us to write down what we felt that God was sharing with us. It was in that moment that the floodgates of heaven opened up. It was as if a dam burst open and my pen took to paper with words pouring out one after another. I could barely keep up with the thoughts that were taking shape into a love letter that was the beginning of a new way I could communicate with God ~ listening and allowing God to share His love with me. As I poured my heart out to Him on paper, He would respond in loving kindness.

I came home and typed up those words, printed them out on fancy paper and bound them in a folder. It felt like one of the greatest gifts I had ever received. I felt loved of God. I felt special. I had received a treasure that deeply touched my heart. This was something I could read and reread whenever I needed love and encouragement. Following that experience, for days on end I would sit and write in journals words that I believed were pouring out from the heart of God.

Several years later as I was going through challenging life events I started writing words of encouragement for others. I would allow the love of God to pour through me in writing so others could be touched by God in a personal way. My dear friend, Robyn Ahearn, would encourage me to write for others while I was undergoing my own trials. She wanted me to focus my attention on giving to others instead of focusing on my struggles. It always worked because I received the greater blessing as I heard back how those who received my words of encouragement were blessed.

I am going to share one of my trials very briefly just touching on the highlights because this book is not a story about me but has been written for the purpose of sharing the love of God to all those who read it.

Due to unfortunate circumstances I was faced with going through a divorce. At that point I had to provide for myself and my children for the first time on my own. I was blessed with a wonderful job but life was a struggle. I was under a great stress load and unexpectedly found myself in the hospital from a manic episode. After coming out of the hospital a second time in two months, I was still sick and unstable. As my manic episode continued, I ended up two states away from home, on the streets with the homeless, and pregnant.

I nearly lost my life a few times along the way but God was watching over me and I eventually made it back home to rebuild my life again. One of the greatest blessings that came out of this particular trial was the birth of my son. He was adopted by a music pastor and her husband, the most amazing parents I could have imagined for my child.

It took some time to crawl back up out of the hole, but God loved me and nurtured me through it all. After much healing and restoration through God's grace, I feel like a whole person and am filled with joy and peace. I spent so many years in need of an encouraging word to get me through my days. My heart's desire was to eventually be able to pour back into others what had been poured into me.

The times I write are precious moments I spend with the Lord. I quietly listen to that still, small voice and words of hope, love, and encouragement pour out as if they are coming straight from the heart of God. His love for us is profound. There are many ways the Lord speaks to us. This book is simply an expression of the love that I believe God holds in His Heart for each and every one of us.

As I was reading one of my writings I had an inspired thought that I should take the writing and turn it around as a mirror image. Doing this brought life to the writings in a new way because it became an interactive dialogue with God where I would listen to Him and then proclaim the words back to Him as an affirmation of His love. I found it so powerful to speak these life giving words over myself. I started reading aloud these affirmations back to God as if in prayer and was strengthened in my spirit by doing so. Therefore, I decided to apply this to all of my writings. It is written as if God is speaking directly to you and then you are repeating the love letter back to Him. It is a simple yet heartfelt dialogue with God ~ a form of prayer.

It is with great joy that I share with you this treasury of faith, hope and love that I believe was inspired by the heart of God. Just sit back and soak in His love as you read. These words were written just for you as well as others. You may read a writing one day and notice certain things speak to you on that day. Then you might revisit that same writing down the road and feel like you are reading it for the first time and that it was meant for you just at that moment in time. The title to each love letter was taken from a phrase within the writing. It is my prayer that these words lift your spirit and bring you the peace of heaven.

For His Glory,
Dana Howard

Romans 15:13 (NLT)

"I pray that God, the source of hope, will fill you completely with joy and peace because you trust in him. Then you will overflow with confident hope through the power of the Holy Spirit."

Table of Contents

1 Corinthians 13:13

And now these three remain: faith, hope and love.

But the greatest of these is love.

1. Seek after me

In the night hours, as you call upon my name, I come running to you. As you awake each morning, the sound of my name upon your lips brings my heart great joy. I want you to know that I consider you my dearest friend, a confidant, one I can share the mysteries of the heavens with as you earnestly seek my face. I want you to understand new things about my love for you. I want you to understand the deepness of my love for you. My love for you has no bounds ~ it is limitless. As far as the eye can see is but a glance in comparison to the vast universe of love I offer to you through my Son. It is through my Son that you have been given new life. It is through my Son's sacrifice on the cross that you have been given a new lease on life, a new opportunity to walk in grace, dignity, and ultimate freedom. Release all your fears and doubts to me and I will pour out upon you life giving words of wisdom that will empower you to walk through your days victoriously. Call upon the name of Jesus, and you shall see walls fall down before you. Call upon the name of Jesus, and you shall see the heavens open up and bring in the new rains of healing and restoration. Be hopeful. Look forward, not behind, for you cannot do anything about what happened yesterday but you can do something new today. You can bring light into this world through me. You are a great light to the world for I am in you and I am light. Seek after me and I will give my all unto you. I will make a way where there seems to be no way. I will part the seas for you and you will walk in a new land with new and greater opportunities to serve your King. Be confident that you have what it takes to be victorious for you have your God on your side. There is nothing that can thwart the plans I have for your life. I have a perfect purpose for your life. **Seek after me** and I will reveal it to you. Know that as you are seeking after me you are always moving forward and never behind. I am at your side at all times, in all circumstances. You are never alone. I am with you always.

I will seek after you

In the night hours, as I call upon your name, you come running to me. As I awake each morning, the sound of your name upon my lips brings your heart great joy. You want me to know that you consider me your dearest friend, a confidant, one you can share the mysteries of the heavens with as I earnestly seek your face. You want me to understand new things about your love for me. You want me to understand the deepness of your love for me. Your love for you has no bounds ~ it is limitless. As far as the eye can see is but a glance in comparison to the vast universe of love you offer to me through your Son. It is through your Son that I have been given new life. It is through your Son's sacrifice on the cross that I have been given a new lease on life, a new opportunity to walk in grace, dignity and ultimate freedom. I will release all my fears and doubts to you and you will pour out upon me life giving words of wisdom that will empower me to walk through my days victoriously. I will call upon the name of Jesus, and I shall see walls fall down before me. I will call upon the name of Jesus, and I shall see the heavens open up and bring in the new rains of healing and restoration. I will be hopeful. I will look forward, not behind, for I cannot do anything about what happened yesterday but I can do something new today. I can bring light into this world through you. I am a great light to the world for you are in me and you are light. I will seek after you and you will give your all unto me. You will make a way where there seems to be no way. You will part the seas for me and I will walk in a new land with new and greater opportunities to serve my King. I will be confident that I have what it takes to be victorious for

*I have my God on my side. There is nothing that can thwart the plans you have for my life. You have a perfect purpose for my life. **I will seek after you** and you will reveal it to me. I will know that as I am seeking after you I am always moving forward and never behind. You are at my side at all times, in all circumstances. I am never alone. You are with me always.*

Deuteronomy 4:29
But if from there you seek the Lord your God,
you will find him if you seek him with all your
heart and with all your soul.

2. You will be lying down in green pastures

When your heart reaches out to me I am reaching out to you. I extend to you all of my love, all of my compassion, all of my grace. In times of trouble do not be afraid for I am with you. The road before you may appear treacherous, but remember, you are not alone. We will take it one step at a time and before you know it **you will be lying down in green pastures** basking in the glory of my light. I am with you to always guide you down the right path. Take time to come away and be with me. This will refresh your spirit and bring joy to your heart on even the most difficult of days. Be patient and trust in me. I will make a way for you in the wilderness and you shall be set free.

I will be lying down in green pastures

When my heart reaches out to you, you are reaching out to me. You extend to me all of your love, all of your compassion, all of your grace. In times of trouble I will not be afraid for you are with me. The road before me may appear treacherous, but I will remember, I am not alone. We will *take it one step at a time and before I know it **I will be lying down in green pastures** basking in the glory of your light. You are with me to always guide me down the right path. I will take time to come away and be with you. This will refresh my spirit and bring joy to my heart on even the most difficult of days. I will be patient and trust in you. You will make a way for me in the wilderness and I shall be set free.*

Psalm 23

The Lord is my shepherd, I lack nothing. He makes me lie down in green pastures, he leads me beside quiet waters, he refreshes my soul. He guides me along the right paths for his name's sake.

3. I will help you to forgive others

I have come so that you may have new life, a life free from bondages. When you feel backed into a corner and you don't know how to escape, call upon my name and I will come running to you. You have felt the wounds that have come from the attacks of the enemy. Talk to me about them. Reach within and express your deepest thoughts and concerns. I sit right by your side and am listening to you. My healing rains, in their mysterious ways, will wash away the hurts and pain. I will help you to sort out your thoughts and bring them into alignment with my will. **I will help you to forgive others** who have hurt you deeply. You will recover and you will become stronger than ever before. Be patient with yourself and listen to the promptings of my spirit which will lead the way. You are closer to freedom than you imagine. I have new blessings awaiting you this day.

You will help me to forgive others

You have come so that I may have new life, a life free from bondages. When I feel backed into a corner and I don't know how to escape, I will call upon your name and you will *come running to me. I have felt the wounds that have come from the attacks of the enemy. I will talk to you about them. I will reach within and express my deepest thoughts and concerns. You sit right by my side and are listening to me. Your healing rains in their mysterious ways will wash away the hurts and pain. You will help me to sort out my thoughts and bring them into alignment with your will. **You will help me to forgive others** who have hurt me deeply. I will recover and I will become stronger than ever before. I will be patient with myself and listen to the promptings of your spirit which will lead the way. I am closer to freedom than I imagine. You have new blessings awaiting me this day.*

Matthew 6:15
But if you do not forgive others their sins, your Father will not forgive your sins.

4. I show myself to you in many ways

My beloved, I call you friend. You can call me friend too. I desire a personal, intimate relationship with you. I want to be your best friend. I want to be your confidant. You can always count on me to listen to you. I will respond in loving kindness. Though you may not hear my voice, I am ever present before you. **I show myself to you in many ways**. Be open to my wisdom that I will impart to you as you come and spend time with me. You will find that as you take the time to be in fellowship with me, your burdens will be lightened and you will receive new strength and a renewed spirit. I am molding you into my image and likeness so that you are a reflection of me to others that I place along your path. Your story will bring hope to others who are lost and broken for they will be witness to the miraculous ways I have moved in your life because of the close friendship we share. Others will desire the same closeness to me and that will draw them into my heart in a new way. Let my light of love shine through you to others. I will be the hope you need to make it through your day. My friend, I love you.

You show yourself to me in many ways

*My Jesus, you call me friend. I can call you friend too. You desire a personal, intimate relationship with me. You want to be my best friend. You want to be my confidant. I can always count on you to listen to me. You will respond in loving kindness. Though I may not hear your voice, you are ever present before me. **You show yourself to me in many ways.** I will be open to your wisdom that you will impart to me as I come and spend time with you. I will find that as I take the time to be in fellowship with you, my burdens will be lightened and I will receive new strength and a renewed spirit. You are molding me into your image and likeness so that I am a reflection of you to others that you place along my path. My story will bring hope to others who are lost and broken for they will be witness to the miraculous ways you have moved in my life because of the close friendship we share. Others will desire the same closeness to you and that will draw them into your heart in a new way. I will let your light of love shine through me to others. You will be the hope I need to make it through my day. My Jesus, I love you.*

John 14:21

Whoever has my commands and keeps them is the one who loves me. The one who loves me will be loved by my Father, and I too will love them and show myself to them.

5. I am a place of refuge for you

In your darkest hours, I am there. In the midst of your pain, I am there. When you think you can't make it through another day, I am there. My love surrounds you and protects you from harm. Release it all to me, your thoughts, your cares, your hurts. I will take them from you to lift the burden from your shoulders as you come to spend time with me. I have many ways of lightening your load that will bring you rest and comfort. When you are too exhausted to even talk to me, just focus your heart on me and I will hold you in my arms. **I am a place of refuge for you** ~ a place where you feel safe and protected. I want to bring you the comfort your heart is longing for. It does not take a lot of effort to come to me and there is such a great reward for you when you do. When you are anxious about how all the details of the day are going to work out, trust in me. Do not fear for I will be with you all the way. I will go before you and orchestrate things on your behalf for the good of all my children. Seek after me and you will find me, even in places you were not expecting. I am near you.

You are a place of refuge for me

*In my darkest hours, you are there. In the midst of my pain, you are there. When I think I can't make it through another day, you are there. Your love surrounds me and protects me from harm. I will release it all to you, my thoughts, my cares, my hurts. You will take them from me to lift the burden from my shoulders as I come to spend time with you. You have many ways of lightening my load that will bring me rest and comfort. When I am too exhausted to even talk to you, I will just focus my heart on you and you will hold me in your arms. **You are a place of refuge for me** ~ a place where I feel safe and protected. You want to bring me the comfort my heart is longing for. It does not take a lot of effort to come to you and there is such a great reward for me when I do. When I am anxious about how all the details of the day are going to work out, I will trust in you. I will not fear for you will be with me all the way. You will go before me and orchestrate things on my behalf for the good of all your children. I will seek after you and I will find you, even in places I was not expecting. You are near me.*

2 Samuel 22:31

As for God, his way is perfect: The Lord's word is flawless; he shields all who take refuge in him.

6. I will love you through this

My sweet and tender heart, I stand right by your side this day and all of your days. When times are uncertain, know that I am here to bring you comfort and strength. As you lift up all your worries and concerns to me, I will take them from you to bring you peace. Let the fire of my love bring you new insight and understanding into the ways I am working within your life despite the trials and tribulations. **I will love you through this**. What you are walking through right now will not break you but will make you stronger and bring you into an even deeper relationship with me. Take hold of my hand and let me lead you beside still waters. You are an overcomer and this is a new opportunity for your strength in me to be an encouragement to others who are also going through the same trials. Stand strong. Be still before me. I am with you.

You will love me through this

Oh sweet and tender Jesus, you stand right by my side this day and all of my days. When times are uncertain, I know that you are here to bring me comfort and strength. As I lift up all my worries and concerns to you, you will take them from me to bring me peace. I will let the fire of your love bring me new insight and understanding into the ways you are working within my life despite the trials and tribulations. **You will love me through this.** *What I am walking through right now will not break me but will make me stronger and bring me into an even deeper relationship with you. I will take hold of your hand and let you lead me beside still waters. I am an overcomer and this is a new opportunity for my strength in you to be an encouragement to others who are also going through the same trials. I will stand strong. I will be still before you. You are with me.*

Psalm 66:12

Then you put a leader over us. We went through fire and flood, but you brought us to a place of great abundance.

7. You are precious in my eyes

My sweet and precious child ~ I am with you today. I am right by your side whispering softly to your spirit to help you process through your thoughts and concerns. I will pour out my wisdom upon you so that you have better direction on how you should proceed. You have a kind and caring heart of which I am well pleased. I know that at times the anguish of your heart overwhelms you. I know that at times you feel as though you can't make it through one more day. I know that you have difficulty understanding why it is taking so long for the promises I speak of to be fulfilled in your life. It is all part of a process of learning and growing so that you can get to a state of total freedom, so that nothing will get in the way of the life giving relationship that I share with you. I am not delayed in answering your prayers. I am right on time. Stand strong in your faith and you will be overwhelmed with the blessings you will receive in times to come. In the present time, rest in my love and continue to give your best each day and I will always bring blessings your way and open your eyes to a greater understanding and awareness of all I am doing in your life. **You are precious in my eyes.** Enjoy your day and remember I am standing right by your side.

I am precious in your eyes

My sweet and precious Jesus ~ you are with me today. You are right by my side whispering softly to my spirit to help me process through my thoughts and concerns. You will pour out your wisdom upon me so that I will have better direction on how I should proceed. I have a kind and caring heart of which you are well pleased. You know that at times the anguish of my heart overwhelms me. You know that at times I feel as though I can't make it through one more day. You know that I have difficulty understanding why it is taking so long for the promises you speak of to be fulfilled in my life. It is all part of a process of learning and growing so that I can get to a state of total freedom, so that nothing will get in the way of the life giving relationship that you share with me. You are not delayed in answering my prayers. You are right on time. I will stand strong in my faith and I will be over-whelmed with the blessings I will receive in times to come. In the present time, I will rest in your love and continue to give my best each day and you will always bring blessings my way and open my eyes to a greater understanding and awareness of all you are doing in my life. **I am precious** *in your eyes. I will enjoy my day and remember you are standing right by my side.*

Daniel 10:19

*"Don't be afraid," he said, "for you are very precious
to God. Peace! Be encouraged! Be strong!"
As he spoke these words to me, I suddenly felt stronger
and said to him, "Please speak to me, my lord,
for you have strengthened me."*

8. I will be faithful to you always

Be near me as I am near you. Stand with me as I stand with you. As you search your heart, you will find within it the greatest treasure ~ my Spirit. I breathe new life into you each day as you reach out to me, as you call upon my name. Oh, my darling child, you honor me when you hold gratitude in your heart for the things I do for you, for the little gifts I send your way just because I love you. Thank you for your thankful heart. What great joy I receive when my children appreciate the love I give in many different ways. Seek me in all that you do and you will find even more reasons to be thankful. In this way as your spirit connects with mine, you will be uplifted up with an enthusiasm to share with others what I have to offer ~ complete and unfailing love. **I will be faithful to you always**, this you can count on.

You will be faithful to me always

I will be near to you as you are near to me. I will stand with you as you stand with me. As I search my heart, I will find within it the greatest treasure ~ your Spirit. You breathe new life into me each day as I reach out to you, as I call upon your name. Oh, my Jesus, I bring honor to you when I hold gratitude in my heart for the things you do for me, for the little gifts you send my way just because you love me. You thank me for my thankful heart. What great joy you receive when your children appreciate the love you give in many different ways. I will seek you in all that I do and I will find even more reasons to be thankful. In this way as my spirit connects with yours, I will be uplifted up with an enthusiasm to share with others what you have to offer ~ complete and unfailing love. **You will be faithful to me always***, this I can count on.*

Deuteronomy 7:9
Know therefore that the LORD **your God is God;**
he is the faithful God, keeping his covenant of love to a
thousand generations of those who love him
and keep his commandments.

9. I have called you according to my purpose

I look upon you, my beloved, and think to myself, what a perfect creation you are. I know the intents of your heart, my child. I see that you are making your best effort at trying to lead a holy and righteous life. Just relax and rest in me. Let me lighten your load, the expectations you put upon yourself for perfection. You know, my beloved, when I see you this day and every day, I behold perfection before my very eyes. You have no idea how greatly you please my heart. You cannot even begin to comprehend how very proud I am of you right now. You so fervently call out to me. You may think you do all the talking, but look here, I see you as a great listener as I am of you. I am your friend, the best and truest you will ever know. You will behold me face to face one day. That is my promise to you. I am giving you the rest you need to recharge your batteries so that you can complete the task I have laid before you. Just as you were pleasantly surprised the other day, so shall I surprise you again in even greater ways. Allow me to fill in the blanks, the missing pieces. I will give you each and every one of them as they are needed, right on time. My love for you reaches the heavens and will never cease for I have always loved you and **I have called you according to my purpose**. Stay the course and you will be well pleased just as I am well pleased with you. Go now and bask in the presence of my Father tonight and you shall find rest. My peace will fall upon you. I love you.

You have called me according to your purpose

You look upon me, your beloved, and think to yourself, what a perfect creation I am. You know the intents of my heart, my Jesus. You see that I am making my best effort at trying to lead a holy and righteous life. I will just relax and rest in you. I will let you lighten my load, the expectations I put upon myself for perfection. I know, my Jesus, when you see me this day and every day, you behold perfection before your very eyes. I have no idea how greatly I please your heart. I cannot even begin to comprehend how very proud you are of me right now. I so fervently call out to you. I may think I do all the talking, but look here, you see me as a great listener as you are of me. You are my friend, the best and truest I will ever know. I will behold you face to face one day. That is your promise to me. You are giving me the rest I need to recharge my batteries so that I can complete the task you have laid before me. Just as I was pleasantly surprised the other day, so shall you surprise me again in even greater ways. I will allow you to fill in the blanks, the missing pieces. You will give me each and every one of them as they are needed, right on time. You love for me reaches the heavens and will never cease for you have always loved me and **you have called me according to your purpose.** *I will stay the course and I will be well pleased just as you are well pleased with me. I will go now and bask in the presence of my Father tonight and I shall find rest. Your peace will fall upon me. I love you.*

Romans 8:28
And we know that all things work together for good
to them that love God, to them who are the called
according to his purpose.

10. I am your shelter during the storms

Dearest beloved child, when you are standing at a cross-road in your life and do not know which way to turn ~ call upon my name. It may be unclear to you now, but I will make the way for you. Do not fear that you will stumble and fall for I am here to protect you. I am the calm within your spirit when times are rough. **I am your shelter during the storms** that can rage about you throughout your days. It will not always be difficult, though it may seem like the battle you are in is never ending. I have come so that you may have rest.

You are my shelter during the storms

*Dearest beloved Jesus, when I am standing at a cross-road in my life and do not know which way to turn ~ I will call upon your name. It may be unclear to me now, but you will make the way for me. I will not fear that I will stumble and fall for you are here to protect me. You are the calm within my spirit when times are rough. **You are my shelter during the storms** that can rage about me throughout my days. It will not always be difficult, though it may seem like* *the battle I am in is never ending. You have come so that I may have rest.*

Psalm 91:1
Whoever dwells in the shelter of the Most High will rest in the shadow of the Almighty.

11. Stand upon my Word

Guard your heart and mind from the attacks of the enemy by proclaiming the truth in my Word. **Stand upon my Word** and rejoice for the promises I speak of are for you too, not just other people. Receive my abundant love this day. If all you can do this moment is read that I love you, that is alright. Let my words be the hope that fills your heart with gladness.

I will stand upon your Word

*I will guard my heart and mind from the attacks of the enemy by proclaiming the truth in your Word. **I will stand upon your Word** and rejoice for the promises you speak of are for me too, not just other people. I will receive your abundant love this day. If all I can do this moment is read that you love me, that is alright. I will let your words be the hope that fills my heart with gladness.*

Psalm 119:89
*Your word, L*ORD*, is eternal; it stands firm in the heavens.*

12. I am working on your behalf

Rest in me. Bring all of your thoughts, concerns and anxieties and lay them at my feet. Submit yourself to me and I will lead you down the right path. Do not weary though the path may seem long and burdensome at times. Let my love strengthen you. I will keep you safe from harm and set up a hedge about you that keeps you walking down the path that leads to freedom, insight, and new revelation into my goodness. Trust in me. Know that **I am working on your behalf** and trailblazing the way for you to walk in truth and righteousness. Seek me and you shall find me even in places you were not expecting. I will be a light to you as you go forth into this new day. Rest in me. I am with you.

You are working on my behalf

I will rest in you. I will bring all of my thoughts, concerns and anxieties and lay them at your feet. I will submit myself to you and you will lead me down the right path. I will not weary though the path may seem long and burdensome at times. I will let your love strengthen me. You will keep me safe from harm and set up a hedge about me that keeps me *walking down the path that leads to freedom, insight, and new revelation into your goodness. I will trust in you. I know that **you are working on my behalf** and trailblazing the way for me to walk in truth and righteousness. I will seek you and I shall find you even in places I was not expecting. You will be a light to me as I go forth into this new day. I will rest in you. You are with me.*

Job 8:6

If you are pure and upright, even now he will rouse himself on your behalf and restore you to your prosperous state.

13. I am refining your spirit and transforming your mind

Sweet child, let me wrap my loving arms around you. Soak in my Spirit within as you rest in me. Did you realize that I was right beside you today? Your confidence is in me and comes through me. You have a light within you that permeates the darkness. I am that light. I am your light. Some days you will be frustrated by the events of the day. All you need to do is continue to press into me. There is no victory without a battle. **I am refining your spirit and transforming your mind.** Do not weary when the challenges of the day fall upon your shoulders. You do not carry them alone although it may seem so at times. Remember, I am training you for battle. I am teaching you how to be victorious. My Word will come alive within you as you call upon my name. Go forth and take new territory! The greater the battle, the greater the victory!

You are refining my spirit and transforming my mind

Sweet Father, I will let you wrap your loving arms around me. I will soak in your Spirit within as I rest in you. I know that you were right beside me today. My confidence is in you and comes through you. I have a light within me that permeates the darkness. You are that light. You are my light. Some days I will be frustrated by the events of the day. All I need to do is continue to press into you. There is no victory without a battle. **You are refining my spirit and transforming my mind.** *I will not weary when the challenges of the day fall upon my shoulders. I do not carry them alone although it may seem so at times. I will remember you are training me for battle. You are teaching me how to be victorious. Your Word will come alive within me as I call upon your name. I will go forth and take new territory! The greater the battle, the greater the victory!*

Romans 12:2
Do not conform to the pattern of this world,
but be transformed by the renewing of your mind.
Then you will be able to test and approve what God's will
is—his good, pleasing and perfect will.

14. My love is sovereign and unyielding

Beloved child, my love is one of the universe's greatest mysteries. I love all of my children equally for each child is my masterpiece created out of the same love, the purest kind of love. **My love is sovereign and unyielding.** It is indeed fathomless. Love shows itself in many different ways. For some, love is experienced in great measure. For others, love has been fleeting. My child, you must remember that this is a fallen world trying to make its way back home. As the end draws near, the fight for good and evil will become stronger and stronger. It is not I who oppresses but he who is in the world. The enemy would have it that all would perish. But I, out of my sovereign love, have overcome the world. What truly matters is not what you experience now in your life. What truly matters is what you will behold in the life to come. Eternal life. You need not understand why life is so complex. All you need to do is to have faith in me. I am the Savior of all. All who believe in me will experience a measure of blessing that is truly out of this world. That measure is saved for those who believe in me and have put their trust in me. I bless you with just one parting truth this day. No matter where you are in life or what you are experiencing, the truth is that I love you. Yes, you are and always will be loved by the one who gave you life.

Your love is sovereign and unyielding

*Beloved Father, your love is one of the universe's greatest mysteries. You love all of your children equally for each child is your masterpiece created out of the same love, the purest kind of love. **Your love is sovereign and unyielding.** It is indeed fathomless. Love shows itself in many different ways. For some, love is experienced in great measure. For others, love has been fleeting. My Father, I must remember that this is a fallen world trying to make its way back home. As the end draws near, the fight for good and evil will become stronger and stronger. It is not you who oppresses but he who is in the world. The enemy would have it that all would perish. But you, out of your sovereign love, have overcome the world. What truly matters is not what I experience now in my life. What truly matters is what I will behold in the life to come. Eternal life. I need not understand why life is so complex. All I need to do is to have faith in you. You are the Savior of all. All who believe in you will experience a measure of blessing that is truly out of this world. That measure is saved*

for those who believe in you and have put their trust in you.
You bless me with just one parting truth this day. No matter
where I am in life or what I am experiencing, the truth is that
you love me. Yes, I am and always will be loved by the one
who gave me life.

Psalm 109:21

But you, Sovereign Lord, help me for your name's sake;
out of the goodness of your love, deliver me.

15. Love me with all of your heart

Oh, how I love you! I pour out my grace upon you this day. How is it that you could fully live without my mercy? It would be impossible for you to grow in true love without my grace. Continue to seek after me. What is your purpose in life? What is your true calling? To **love me with all of your heart** and with all of your soul and with all of your strength and with all your mind. And yes, to love others as you love yourself. Hope in me, my child, and know that your hope in me will not disappoint you. The trials that you go through are for the good of your soul. They serve to mature and grow you in love. I am your master just as you are my servant. I am the greatest teacher you will ever know. Come to me even when you are weary and I will give you rest. Delight in me and I will give you the desires of your heart!

I will love you with all of my heart

Oh, how you love me! You pour out your grace upon me this day. How is it that I could fully live without your mercy? It would be impossible for me to grow in true love without your grace. I will continue to seek after you. What is my purpose in life? What is my true calling? To **love you with all of my heart** and with all of my soul and with all of my strength and with all my mind. And yes, to love others as I love myself. I will hope in you, my Father, and know that my hope in you will not disappoint me. The trials that I go through are for the good of my soul. They serve to mature and grow me in love. You are my master just as I am your servant. You are the greatest teacher I will ever know. I will come to you even when I am weary and you will give me rest. I will delight in you and you will give me the desires of my heart!

Luke 10:27

He answered, 'Love the Lord your God with all your heart and with all your soul and with all your strength and with all your mind'; and, 'Love your neighbor as yourself.'

16. I will guide your every step

My dear child, you are brave indeed. You have boldly taken on new challenges that I have placed before you. As you continue to put your trust in me and seek my guidance, I will be with you to help you endure any trials that come your way. These challenges are for the good of your soul and will propel you forward to places you have never even dreamed of. I want to show you my goodness and my faithfulness. I know that you are seeking my promise and I want you to rest assured that the time is drawing nearer than you can imagine. Enjoy the journey. You will be able to look back on the trials of your journey and come to understand why I allowed you to go through them. You were not only called to be my servant, you were called to be my Bride. You will stand before me in righteousness, purity and wholeness with the fullness of my Spirit within you. Continue to press into me as you have been doing. Seek after my truth and **I will guide your every step** and give you great knowledge and understanding of my love for you and why I suffered on the cross for you. I am pleased with you and look upon you with great love and admiration. I am proud of you. Keep steadfast and true to my calling for your life that I will reveal to you in the days to come. Rest now and be comforted in my presence. New joy will be with you when you arise. A new day is dawning and my angels will be watching over you as you rest in peace.

You will guide my every step

My dear Father, I am brave indeed. I have boldly taken on new challenges that you have placed before me. As I continue to put my trust in you and seek your guidance, you will be with me to help me endure any trials that come my way. These challenges are for the good of my soul and will propel me forward to places I have never even dreamed of. You want to show me your goodness and your faithfulness. You know that I am seeking your promise and you want me to rest assured that the time is drawing nearer than I can imagine. I will enjoy the journey. I will be able to look back on the trials of my journey and come to understand why you allowed me to go through them. I was not only called to be your servant, I was called to be your Bride. I will stand before you in righteousness, purity and wholeness with the fullness of your Spirit within me. I will continue to press into you as I have been doing. I will seek after your truth and you will guide my every step and give me great knowledge and understanding of your love for me and why you suffered on the cross for me. You are pleased with me and look upon me with great love and admiration. You are proud of me. I will keep steadfast and true to your calling for my life that you will reveal to me in the days to come. I will rest now and be comforted in your presence. New joy will be with me when I arise. A new day is dawning and your angels will be watching over me as I rest in peace.

Exodus 15:13
In your unfailing love you will lead the people
you have redeemed. In your strength you will guide them
to your holy dwelling.

17. Jesus, you are my rock

*My Lord and my God I thank you. I thank you for giving me life. I thank you for giving me the opportunity to love you. I thank you for your patience with me as I grow and learn. I may fall but with your help I always rise again. I thank you for the trials. Through the trials I have built character through perseverance. I may walk through the fire but I will not be burned for you will save me. **You are my rock**, my firm foundation.*

Deuteronomy 32:4
He is the Rock, his works are perfect,
and all his ways are just. A faithful God who does
no wrong, upright and just is he.

18. I will carry you

My humble child, be not weary for I am your helper in times of need. I have not forgotten you, on the contrary, you are always on the forefront of my mind. You cannot always see the end from the beginning but know this, my plans for you are wonderful. What you are lacking now, you will be overflowing with in times to come. My arms are around you this day, to comfort, to guide and protect you. Try your best to not let the enemy's lies bring you down. He will try to overwhelm you with thoughts of inadequacies and failures. These are lies. The truth is that you are my child for whom all my goodness flows. You are full of my goodness and my grace is sufficient for you even on days when you are heavy laden and sorrowful. I hear the cries of your heart and my heart is filled with compassion for you. My love for you abounds. You are a precious soul, so perfectly created by me and you are indeed the apple of my eye. All will be well, my beloved. You are esteemed in the kingdom of heaven and I have called you to higher ground. You have been walking up the steep mountain path and the journey has been wearisome. As you continue to draw on my strength, **I will carry you** the rest of the way up the mountain. From the top you will look below and will come to understand how I have been cultivating your heart in holiness. From the mountain top you will see things as you have never seen them and all that you have learned on this rocky, steep path will bubble over and pour out as wisdom that will empower you to bring healing to those who are lost and broken. The end of this path is in sight. It only takes a gust of wind to move the clouds that block your view of the mountain top. My Spirit is blowing gently and perfectly upon your path and you will behold my majesty in new and creative ways in days to come. Draw into my arms and let me shelter you. I have come so that you may have rest. I bring peace and help to you this day. All will be well. I love you.

You will carry me

My Jesus, I will not be weary for you are my helper in times of need. You have not forgotten me, on the contrary, I am always on the forefront of your mind. I cannot always see the end from the beginning but I will know this, your plans for me are wonderful. What I am lacking now, I will be overflowing with in times to come. Your arms are around me this day, to comfort, to guide and protect me. I will try my best to not let the enemy's lies bring me down. He will try to overwhelm me with thoughts of inadequacies and failures. These are lies. The truth is that I am your child for whom all your goodness flows. I am full of your goodness and your grace is sufficient for me even on days when I am heavy laden and sorrowful. You hear the cries of my heart and your heart is filled with compassion for me. Your love for me abounds. I am a precious soul, so perfectly created by you and I am indeed the apple of your eye. All will be well, my Jesus. I am esteemed in the kingdom of heaven and you have called me to higher ground. I have been walking up the steep mountain path and the journey has been wearisome. As I continue to draw on your strength, **you will carry me** the rest of the way up the mountain. From the top I will look below and will come to understand how you have been cultivating my heart in holiness. From the mountain top I will see things as I have never seen them and all that I have learned on this rocky, steep path will bubble over and pour out as wisdom that will empower me to bring healing to those who are lost and broken. The end of this path is in sight. It only takes a gust of wind to move the clouds that block my view of the mountain top. Your Spirit is blowing gently and perfectly upon my path and I will behold your majesty in new and creative ways in *days to come. I will draw into your arms and let you shelter me. You have come so that I may have rest. You bring peace and help to me this day. All will be well. You love me.*

Psalm 28:9

Save your people and bless your inheritance; be their shepherd and carry them forever.

19. I am holding onto you

I stand beside you this night to listen to you, to hear your thoughts. There is no time or place that I am not with you. I am with you always. You may have lost your footing for a moment and slipped. You are going to be just fine for **I am holding onto you**. Just because you have stumbled does not mean you have fallen. On the contrary, this incident has served its purpose to bring you back into my arms where you belong. I have been patiently waiting for your arrival. All you need to do is knock and I will open up the door to my heart where we can discuss your circumstances in the safety of my loving presence. I cherish you and am so proud to call you my beloved child. You have not disappointed me. The fact that you are with me now brings great joy to my heart. I have been waiting for this special moment in time to speak directly to your spirit. My love for you abounds, my child. Never forget the fact that I never forget about you. You are always in my heart and on my mind. Rest this night in the comfort of my love. I will be with you as you sleep and will greet you when you arise in the morning. I will be with you tomorrow and will help you. Sweet dreams, my child.

You are holding onto me

*You stand beside me this night to listen to me, to hear my thoughts. There is no time or place that you are not with me. You are with me always. I may have lost my footing for a moment and slipped. I am going to be just fine for **you are holding onto me**. Just because I have stumbled does not mean I have fallen. On the contrary, this incident has served its purpose to bring me back into your arms where I belong. You have been patiently waiting for my arrival. All I need to do is knock and you will open up the door to your heart where we can discuss my circumstances in the safety of your loving presence. You cherish me and are so proud to call me your beloved child. I have not disappointed you. The fact that I am with you now brings great joy to your heart. You have been waiting for this special moment in time to speak directly to my spirit. Your love for me abounds, my Jesus. I will never forget the fact that you never forget about me. I am always in your heart and on your mind. I will rest this night in the comfort of your love. You will be with me as I sleep and will greet me when I arise in the morning. You will be with me tomorrow and will help me. Sweet dreams, my Jesus.*

Deuteronomy 11:22-23

If you carefully observe all these commands I am giving you to follow—to love the Lord your God, to walk in obedience to him and to hold fast to him— then the Lord will drive out all these nations before you, and you will dispossess nations larger and stronger than you.

20. I will give you what you need

As you reach out to me in prayer, I am reaching out to you. Do not worry about how every little detail is going to work out. The tapestry of your life is being woven by me and even the tiniest piece of thread is not overlooked but strategically placed exactly where it needs to be. Allow me to tend to the details for you. Simply trust in your Provider and **I will give you what you need**, exactly how and when you need it. Be mindful to rest in me. Keep your hope alive within you by proclaiming my promises that I speak of so many times in my Word. When you speak these truths they will manifest in your life in the perfect time, not too late, not too early. I am a God of perfection and I am weaving my glory and promises into the tapestry of your life each day. Stay the course and keep your eyes fixed on me. I am making the way for you. Victory is in the making and joy is on its wings!

You will give me what I need

As I reach out to you in prayer, you are reaching out to me. I will not worry about how every little detail is going *to work out. The tapestry of my life is being woven by you and even the tiniest piece of thread is not overlooked but strategically placed exactly where it needs to be. I will allow you to tend to the details for me. I will simply trust in my Provider and **you will give me what I need**, exactly how and when I need it. I will be mindful to rest in you. I will keep my hope alive within me by proclaiming your promises that you speak of so many times in your Word. When I speak these truths they will manifest in my life in the perfect time, not too late, not too early. You are a God of perfection and you are weaving your glory and promises into the tapestry of my life each day. I will stay the course and keep my eyes fixed on you. You are making the way for me. Victory is in the making and joy is on its wings!*

2 Peter 1:3

His divine power has given us everything we need for a godly life through our knowledge of him who called us by his own glory and goodness.

21. Sit at my feet

Sit at my feet and listen to me. Listen to the gentle words of love that I pour upon you this hour. As you receive my love, be open to the transformational powers of my undying love for you. It is not my perfect plan that you should struggle or battle through life but that is the way of the world. It is my perfect plan that you continue to put your faith and trust in me. By doing that, my spirit will come alive within your heart and you will reap the benefits that I pour out upon my children who believe in me. I am with you today and all of your days.

I will sit at your feet

I will sit at your feet and listen to you. I will listen to the gentle words of love that you pour upon me this hour. As I receive your love, I will be open to the transformational powers of your undying love for me. It is not your perfect plan that I should struggle or battle through life but that is the way of the world. It is your perfect plan that I continue to put my faith and hope in you. By doing that, your Spirit will come alive within my heart and I will reap the benefits that you pour out upon your children who believe in you. You are with me today and all of my days.

Luke 10:38-39

As Jesus and his disciples were on their way, he came to a village where a woman named Martha opened her home to him. She had a sister called Mary, who sat at the Lord's feet listening to what he said.

22. My light is upon you

Dearest child, I beckon you to call upon my name. Come before me so that I may see your face. Let me uncover your hurts and pains and bring you comfort that is true and lasting. You may be facing something today that is greater than what you thought you could handle. This is the battle of life. Some days you will feel stronger than others. Today, remember that when you are weak, I am strong. I will carry you through this dark hour and bring you to the other side that is full of light and hope. You are much stronger than you think you are. I have overcome so that you too may overcome. My light breaks through the darkness and casts away shadows and things lurking in dark corners. **My light is upon you**. Let me be your strength, the strength that carries you through the day. I am with you.

Your light is upon me

Dearest Jesus, you beckon me to call upon your name. I will come before you so that you may see my face. I will let you uncover my hurts and pains and you will bring me comfort that is true and lasting. I am facing something today *that is greater than what I thought I could handle. This is the battle of life. Some days I will feel stronger than others. Today, I will remember that when I am weak, you are strong. You will carry me through this dark hour and bring me to the other side that is full of light and hope. I am much stronger than I think I am. You have overcome so that I too may overcome. Your light breaks through the darkness and casts away shadows and things lurking in dark corners. **Your light is upon me**. I will let you be my strength, the strength that carries me through the day. You are with me.*

Isaiah 60:1
Arise, shine, for your light has come,
and the glory of the Lord rises upon you.

23. The depth of my love

Oh, that you would know **the depth of my love** for you! My love for you is fathomless. It is incomprehensible. It is so great that I created a universe that is never ending just to give you a glimpse of the love I hold in my heart just for you. And yet, even a never ending universe cannot contain my love. My love for you is infinite. My heart is infinite and contains so much love that I created time without end so that I could love you for eternity. My love for you will never cease. Your comprehension of my love is like one grain of sand in ten thousand planets, yet that does not even begin to compare to the love I hold in my heart for you. You are never outside of my love. When you do not feel my love, it is not because it is not there, for my love for you is constant. My love was, is and ever shall be. Although you are limited in your understanding of how much I love you, know that I do. I do all things out of love for you. Just as you cannot comprehend the depths to which I love you, you will not always understand why I do what I do. Just know and remember, as I speak of in My Word, that my thoughts are higher than your thoughts and my ways are higher than your ways. What I do, I do because I love you. Today, as you ponder on my love, rest assured that I will give you what you need to make it through the day no matter what it holds. Hold onto this one thought today ~ I love you.

The depth of your love

*Oh, that I would know **the depth of your love** for me! Your love for me is fathomless. It is incomprehensible. It is so great that you created a universe that is never ending just to give me a glipmse of the love you hold in your heart just for me. And yet, even a never ending universe cannot contain your love. Your love for me is infinite. Your heart is infinite and contains so much love that you created time without end so that you could love me for eternity. Your love for me will never cease. My comprehension of your love is like one grain of sand in ten thousand planets, yet that does not even begin to compare to the love you hold in your heart for me. I am never outside of your love. When I do not feel your love, it is not because it is not there, for your love for me is constant. Your love was, is and ever shall be. Although I am limited in my understanding of how much you love me, I will know that you do. You do all things out of love for me. Just as I cannot comprehend the depths to which you love* *me, I will not always understand why you do what you do. I just know and remember, as you speak of in your Word, that your thoughts are higher than my thoughts and your ways are higher than my ways. What you do, you do because you love me. Today, as I ponder on your love, I will rest assured that you will give me what I need to make it through the day no matter what it holds. I will hold onto this one thought today ~ you love me.*

Ephesians 3:16-21

I pray that out of his glorious riches he may strengthen you with power through his Spirit in your inner being, so that Christ may dwell in your hearts through faith. And I pray that you, being rooted and established in love, may have power, together with all the Lord's holy people, to grasp how wide and long and high and deep is the love of Christ, and to know this love that surpasses knowledge—that you may be filled to the measure of all the fullness of God.

24. I am standing with you

Stand strong, my child! I am your covering. I am your protective shield. You are not alone in this battle. **I am standing with you**. When you feel lost, call upon my name. When you feel afraid, come and hide in my arms. When you feel bewildered, seek my Word. My truth shall make a way for you always ~ the way of righteousness.

You are standing with me

*I will stand strong, my Jesus! You are my covering. You are my protective shield. I am not alone in this battle. **You are standing with me**. When I feel lost I will call upon your name. When I feel afraid I will come and hide in your arms. When I feel bewildered I will seek your Word. Your truth shall make a way for me always ~ the way of righteousness.*

Psalm 73:23
Yet I am always with you; you hold me by my right hand.

25. The fire of my love protects you from harm

The fire of my love burns within your heart this day to give you strength. **The fire of my love protects you from harm**. It keeps the pestilence out and refines your walk toward holiness. As the fire of my love is all around you, you are empowered to stand strong against the enemy so that you are able to live a life that is full of my riches and wealth. The kind of wealth that I speak of is the riches that are stored in the treasury of your heart where I reside. I make deposits into the treasury of your heart each time you call upon my name, every time you reach out to someone in need, every moment you spend in worship before the Father. Let the fire of my love light your heart on fire with love and passion for the one who has given you life. I have come so that you may have life and have it in abundance.

The fire of your love protects me from harm

*The fire of your love burns within my heart this day to give me strength. **The fire of your love protects me from harm**. It keeps the pestilence out and refines my walk toward holiness. As the fire of your love is all around me, I am* *empowered to stand strong against the enemy so that I am able to live a life that is full of your riches and wealth. The kind of wealth that you speak of is the riches that are stored in the treasury of my heart where you reside. You make deposits into the treasury of my heart each time I call upon your name, every time I reach out to someone in need, every moment I spend in worship before the Father. Let the fire of your love light my heart on fire with love and passion for the one who has given me life. You have come so that I may have life and have it in abundance.*

Psalm 5:11
**But let all who take refuge in you be glad;
let them ever sing for joy. Spread your protection over
them, that those who love your name may rejoice in you.**

26. Count this day as a victory

Oh, great joy you are to my heart! Look at all that I am doing in your life. You are an overcomer through me. It takes effort on your part to be an overcomer and with your effort comes my blessing. Strive to do your very best, to give all you have, to pour your heart into the lives of others that I have put in your midst. As I bring those people to you, I will also give you the wisdom you need to bring hearts closer to me and for some, to bring them into my heart for the very first time. I am working within you to bring life to others through me. Take another step on your journey today and **count this day as a victory**. Rejoice, for tomorrow will be another victory as you put all your trust in me.

I will count this day as a victory

Oh, great joy you are to my heart! I look at all that you are doing in my life. I am an overcomer through you. It takes effort on my part to be an overcomer and with my effort comes your blessing. I will strive to do my very best, to give all I have, to pour my heart into the lives of others that you have put in my midst. As you bring those people to me, you

82

*will also give me the wisdom I need to bring hearts closer to you and for some, to bring them into your heart for the very first time. You are working within me to bring life to others through you. I will take another step on my journey today and **count this day as a victory**. I will rejoice, for tomorrow will be another victory as I put all my trust in you.*

Deuteronomy 20:4

For the LORD** your God is the one who goes with you to fight for you against your enemies to give you victory."**

27. The glory of this present house

You are a walking testimony that does not hold back from pouring hope into the lives of others. Every prayer uttered by your lips and said quietly within your heart is heard by me. I am a God that answers those who are faithful and diligent in their pursuit for holiness. Wisdom, sweet beautiful wisdom ~ it is yours ~ all you need to do is ask. Over and over I have heard the cries of your heart. Your years of hardship were not in vain and **the glory of this present house will be greater than the glory of the former one**. May your hope stand strong, for I am not a God that will disappoint. I may not answer in your timing, but in my perfect timing. My plans for you are perfect and each answer is delivered at the perfect time. Sing unto my heart and I will sing unto your heart. Rest in my love for it is yours and I give it to you pressed down, shaken together, and overflowing.

The glory of this present house

I am a walking testimony that does not hold back from pouring hope into the lives of others. Every prayer uttered by my lips and said quietly within my heart is heard by you. You are a God that answers those who are faithful and diligent in their pursuit for holiness. Wisdom, sweet beautiful wisdom ~ it is mine ~ all I need to do is ask. Over and over you have heard the cries of my heart. My years of hardship were not in vain and **the glory of this present house will be greater than the glory of the former one**. May my hope stand strong, for you are not a God that will disappoint. You may not answer in my timing, but in your perfect timing. Your plans for me are perfect and each answer is delivered at the perfect time. I will sing unto your heart and you will sing unto my heart. I will rest in your love for it is mine and you give it to me pressed down, shaken together, and overflowing.

Haggai 2:9

'The glory of this present house will be greater than the glory of the former house,' says the Lord Almighty.
'And in this place I will grant peace,'
declares the Lord Almighty."

28. Keep your eyes focused on me

This day, lift up your heart to me. I take your heart in my hand and cleanse it with my love. As my love cleanses your heart, your spirit will be refreshed and you will walk again in purity before me. **Keep your eyes focused on me** and I will be your great reward. Remember, as you have asked for forgiveness, I have cleansed your heart. You are free. Go now and rejoice, for it is a new day. Expect the miraculous. I have so much to give to you. Open your heart to receive my love and you will be greatly blessed.

I will keep my eyes focused on you

This day, I will lift up my heart to you. You take my heart in your hand and cleanse it with your love. As your love cleanses my heart, my spirit will be refreshed and I will walk again in purity before you. ***I will keep my eyes focused on you*** *and you will be my great reward. I will remember, as I have asked for forgiveness, you have cleansed my heart. I am free. I will go now and rejoice, for it is a new day. I will expect the miraculous. You have so much to give to* me. *I will open my heart to receive your love and I will be greatly blessed.*

Psalm 141:8

But my eyes are fixed on you, Sovereign Lord;

in you I take refuge—do not give me over to death.

29. You are always a new creation in me

Dearest child, you are beloved of my heart. I long to give you all the desires of your heart. I long to see you grow deeper and deeper in love with me. My love for you is deep and wide. My mighty hand is upon you. I stand before the throne of my Father pleading on your behalf that you will always be keen to heed my voice ~ to make right choices in the midst of a fallen world. When you are with me, you are on the right path that leads to righteousness and holiness. I will quiet the noises that distract you. I will place a muffle upon your ears that creates a cushion and has a dampening effect to the many voices that can easily toss you to and fro. You will hear my voice loud and clear without distraction. My voice will lead you gently throughout your days and will keep you pliable to the molding and transformational power of my love. When you are in doubt hearken to hear my voice. When you are in doubt be still and know that I am God, not just any God, but the God, your God. I have the power to save. I have the power to redeem. I have the power to heal. I have the power to restore. I will restore you. I will refresh you. I will empower you. I will feed you. I will nourish you. I will protect you. I will transform you. I will hold you always in my loving arms. You will never be the same again because **you are always a new creation in me**.

I am always a new creation in you

Dearest Jesus, I am beloved of your heart. You long to give me all the desires of my heart. You long to see me grow deeper and deeper in love with you. Your love for me is deep and wide. Your mighty hand is upon me. You stand before the throne of your Father pleading on my behalf that I will always be keen to heed your voice ~ to make right choices in the midst of a fallen world. When I am with you, I am on the right path that leads to righteousness and holiness. You quiet the noises that distract me. You place a muffle upon my ears that creates a cushion and has a dampening effect to the many voices that can easily toss me to and fro. I will hear your voice loud and clear without distraction. Your voice will lead me gently throughout my days and will keep me pliable to the molding and transformational power of your love. When I am in doubt I will hearken to hear your voice. When I am in doubt I will be still and know that you are God, not just any God, but the God, my God. You have the power to save. You have the power to redeem. You have the power to *heal. You have the power to restore. You will restore me. You will refresh me. You will empower me. You will feed me. You will nourish me. You will protect me. You will transform me. You will hold me always in your loving arms. I will never be the same again because **I am always a new creation in you**.*

2 Corinthians 5:17

Therefore, if anyone is in Christ, the new creation has come: The old has gone, the new is here!

30. Go forth and sing a new song

You are a fragrant aroma to my heart. Your whispers of love directed toward my heart fill my throne room with such a sweet and pleasing fragrance. Stand strong today! Be brave and courageous! In the midst of trials and tribulations come many victories, big and small. I am with you to guide you and direct your every step as you call upon my name and seek direction for your life. Your obedience to follow my Word and stand on my precepts will go far in my Kingdom. Let your light shine at all times ~ my light of love within you. **Go forth and sing a new song** unto your King who is proud to call you, friend.

I will go forth and sing a new song

I am a fragrant aroma to your heart. My whispers of love directed toward your heart fill your throne room with such a sweet and pleasing fragrance. I will stand strong today! I will be brave and courageous! In the midst of trials and tribulations come many victories, big and small. You are with me to guide me and direct my every step as I call upon your name and seek direction for my life. My obedience to follow your Word and stand on your precepts will go far in your Kingdom. I will let your light shine at all times ~ your light of love within me. **I will go forth and sing a new song** unto my King who is proud to call me, friend.

Psalm 98:1

Sing to the Lord a new song, for he has done marvelous things; his right hand and his holy arm have worked salvation for him.

31. You are wrapped in my loving arms

All you need to do is reach out to me and I will take you by the hand and lead you beside still waters. Be encouraged and know this, **you are wrapped in my loving arms** and I will never let you go. Take a step out of the boat and walk with me upon the waters. Do not be afraid for as I speak peace over your life, so will there be peace. Why is it that the journey seems so long and arduous, you ask? The pathway to living in the fullness of my presence is narrow. It is my job to help refine you and present you before my Father as holy and blameless.

I am wrapped in your loving arms

*All I need to do is reach out to you and you will take me by the hand and lead me beside still waters. I will be encouraged and know this, **I am wrapped in your loving arms** and you will never let me go. I will take a step out of the boat and walk with you upon the waters. I will not be afraid for as you speak peace over my life, so will there be peace. Why is it that the journey seems so long and arduous? The pathway to living in the fullness of your presence is narrow. It is your* *job to help refine me and present me before our Father as holy and blameless.*

Isaiah 40:11

**He tends his flock like a shepherd: He gathers
the lambs in his arms and carries them close to his heart;
he gently leads those that have young.**

32. Jesus, you are my everything

My God, where are you now? My innermost being knows that you are with me yet I do not feel you. I feel as though I am walking alone on this journey. Why is that, oh Lord? Why is the burden of this day so heavy? Show me your way and feed me your truth for I need nourishment for my soul. How can I withstand this weight upon my shoulders? I cannot do it alone so I fervently call upon your name. You are quick to answer for you know that I need you. Thank you for the comfort you bring when my heart is weary. With you I am strong. Without you I am nothing. Teach me, my Lord, so that I may be a light that shines brightly bringing hope to others who are lost and broken. I am not the only one undergoing trials. I am not alone for you are with me. You are my light. **Jesus, you are my everything.**

Luke 15:31
My son, the father said, you are always with me,
and everything I have is yours.

33. I am pleased with you

Beloved child, you radiate today with a joy that comes from within, my Spirit of joy. Within you I shine a light into the darkness to bring a fullness of light. Just as a shepherd keeps his sheep, so shall you find the lost and broken hearted and speak to their hearts with love and compassion. Never have I been so proud to call you my beloved child. You are radiant and stand out among many brethren. I see a great light in you, one that burns brightly from dawn to dusk. When I call upon your name, my child, your heart is turned toward me. When I speak softly and gently to you, you hear my voice and heed my wisdom. This life of yours is but nothing in comparison to the eternal glory you will experience when I call you home. You have laid your life down for me. Oh, that you could see what I have in store for you! You shall not be disappointed. You shall rejoice. You will wake up each day with a new fervor to serve your Master and King. My child of grace ~ I love you. **I am pleased with you**, with your sacrificial life of giving to others without expecting anything in return ~ doing it all out of obedience to your Lord and Savior. Nothing you do or say or think goes unnoticed by me. I will meet all of your needs. Yes, I will meet all of your needs. Beloved child, there is a song in your heart. Sing it forth and believe it! The song pouring forth from your heart is my song to you.

You are pleased with me

*Beloved Jesus, I radiate today with a joy that comes from within, your Spirit of joy. Within me you shine a light into the darkness to bring a fullness of light. Just as a shepherd keeps his sheep, so shall I find the lost and broken hearted and speak to their hearts with love and compassion. Never have you been so proud to call me your beloved child. I am radiant and stand out among many brethren. You see a great light in me, one that burns brightly from dawn to dusk. When you call upon my name, my Jesus, my heart is turned toward you. Even when you speak softly and gently to me, I hear your voice and heed your wisdom. This life of mine is but nothing in comparison to the eternal glory I will experience when you call me home. I have laid my life down for you. Oh, that I could see what you have in store for me! I shall not be disappointed. I shall rejoice. I will wake up each day with a new fervor to serve my Master and King. I am your child of grace and you love me. **You are pleased with me**,* with my sacrificial life of giving to others without expecting anything in return ~ doing it all out of obedience to my Lord and Savior. Nothing I do or say or think goes unnoticed by you. You will meet all of my needs. Yes, you will meet all of my needs. Beloved Jesus, there is a song in my heart. I will sing it forth and believe it! The song pouring forth from my heart is your song to me.

Exodus 33:13

If you are pleased with me, teach me your ways so I may know you and continue to find favor with you. Remember that this nation is your people.

34. I will be there to help and guide you

Beloved child of my heart, I am with you to the end. I am in the midst of all your circumstances. I am a shield about you. Never once do I slumber when it comes to looking after you. I keep a watchful eye upon you at all times. Think of a storm. I stand in the eye of the storm, the peaceful center, that place where you can be with me in the midst of the storm as you give all your anxieties to me. I am the peacemaker. I go ahead of you on your behalf and clear any pathway that may be obstructing your advancement in my Kingdom. Let me take you by the hand and lead you up a new path to the mountain top, to a new level where I can speak to you in those quiet places where you rest with me. Upon the mountain you shall see things at a new vantage point. At times the winds blow and the clouds sweep in so that as you are scaling the mountain, you can no longer see the mountain top. It is in those times you need to put all your trust in me; for as you do, I will take position in your life as your mountain guide. You do not have to see the end from the beginning to continue upward on your journey. I am always there right beside you. At times you will feel confident enough to climb and move forward on your own as you walk in my wisdom. At other times, you will need to hold my hand. Wherever you are on your journey, **I will be there to help and guide you**. I am calling you to the mountain top where you will be able to see things the way I see things and receive new wisdom, insight and understanding. Come forth! Be courageous! Be encouraged! Come and follow me and I shall give you rest.

I will be there to help and guide you

Beloved Jesus, you are with me to the end. You are in the midst of all my circumstances. You are a shield about me. Never once do you slumber when it comes to looking after me. You keep a watchful eye upon me at all times. I will think of a storm. You stand in the eye of the storm, the peaceful center, that place where I can be with you in the midst of the storm as I give all my anxieties to you. You are the peacemaker. You go ahead of me on my behalf and clear any pathway that may be obstructing my advancement in your Kingdom. I will let you take me by the hand and lead me up a new path to the mountain top, to a new level where you can speak to me in those quiet places where I rest with you. Upon the mountain I shall see things at a new vantage point. At times the winds blow and the clouds sweep in so that as I am scaling the mountain, *I can no longer see the mountain top. It is in those times I need to put all my trust in you; for as I do, you will take position in my life as my mountain guide. I do not have to see the end from the beginning to continue upward on my journey. You are always there right beside me. At times I will feel confident enough to climb and move forward on my own as I walk in your wisdom. At other times, I will need to hold your hand. Wherever I am on my journey, **you will be there to help and guide me**. You are calling me to the mountain top where I will be able to see things the way you see things and receive new wisdom, insight and understanding. I will come forth! I will be courageous! I will be encouraged! I will come and follow you and you shall give me rest.*

Psalm 139:10
Even there your hand will guide me,
your right hand will hold me fast.

35. I love you beyond compare

Dearest child, **I love you beyond compare**. Stand strong amidst the storms of life. You will prevail for I am with you. Be strong today and remember I am with you. When you feel lost, call upon my name. When you feel afraid, come and hide in my arms. When you feel bewildered, seek my Word. My truth shall make a way for you always, the way of righteousness.

You love me beyond compare

*Dearest Jesus, **you love me beyond compare**. I will stand strong amidst the storms of life. I will prevail for you are with me. I will be strong today and remember you are with me. When I feel lost, I will call upon your name. When I feel afraid, I will come and hide in your arms. When I feel bewildered, I will seek your Word. Your truth shall make a way for me always, the way of righteousness.*

Psalm 36:7
How priceless is your unfailing love, O God! People take refuge in the shadow of your wings.

36. I will give you rest as you call upon my name

My child, lift up your eyes to your Maker and know that I am God. I will always be with you in your time of need. I am your comforter and protector. As the storms of life rage, I am the one who calms the storm. Release your fears and take my hand. You need not worry for I am here to take care of you. As you sleep, angels are singing my praises in your presence so that you are drawn into the heavens in your spirit. As you awake, I set my angels about you to guard and protect you. There is a song in the heavens with your name on it ~ it is the song of your heart that cries out to me, "Lord God help me, I love you, and I need you now more than ever." I hear your cries, the love song of your heart and my heart is turned with compassion toward you. Let me soothe you with my tenderness toward you. Receive my grace and mercy, the glimpses of joy that spark in your heart even amidst the storm. Hold onto the little tender mercies I send your way, for they shall give you the strength you need to make it through each day. I am the Healer. Healing that takes place starts within the heart first. Even in sickness, your heart can grow stronger and your praises sing louder. Take this time of adversity and rest completely in me. **I will give you rest as you call upon my name**. Sweet songs of love are pouring over you ~ sweet songs of joy are coming your way. Sweet songs of love I sing to you every day. I am with you every moment. You are never alone.

You will give me rest

My Jesus, I will lift up my eyes to my Maker and know that you are God. You will always be with me in my time of need. You are my comforter and protector. As the storms of life rage, you are the one who calms the storm. I will release my fears and take your hand. I need not worry for you are here to take care of me. As I sleep, angels are singing your praises in my presence so that I am drawn into the heavens in my spirit. As I awake, you set your angels about me to guard and protect me. There is a song in the heavens with my name on it ~ it is the song of my heart that cries out to you, "Lord God help me, I love you, and I need you now more than ever." You hear my cries, the love song of my heart and your heart is turned with compassion toward me. I will let you soothe me with your tenderness toward me. I will receive your grace and mercy, the glimpses of joy that spark in my heart even amidst the storm. I will hold onto the little tender mercies you send my way, for they shall give me the strength I need to make it through each day. You are the Healer. Healing that takes place starts within the heart first. Even in sickness, my heart can grow stronger and my praises sing louder. I will take this time of adversity and rest completely in you. **You will give me rest as I call upon your name** ~ *sweet songs of love are pouring over me. Sweet songs of joy are coming my way. Sweet songs of love you sing to me every day. You are with me every moment. I am never alone.*

Matthew 11:28
Come to me, all you who are weary and burdened, and I will give you rest.

37. Hold onto the hope I have given you

Sweet child, how I long to have you sit in my presence and soak in my majesty. You are wonderful in the sight of your Maker. You have made tremendous strides in your journey to my heart. You are an overcomer. With me you are victorious. Your life shall bring glory to my name. I care for all your needs, big and small. I am your protector. I am your great provider. No one shall thwart the plans I have for your life for I have called you by name. You are mine. You are chosen. You belong to the Almighty One. Songs of deliverance and freedom are flowing down from the heavens above to rest upon your heart this day. Receive this music as a sweet comfort to your heart. Joy in great measure I am giving to you, my child. Righteousness and truth is presiding over your heart and mind. Wisdom into the things that are incomprehensible will give you new insight and revelation. Listen to that still, small voice within your heart that tells you which way to turn at every crossroad in your life. Pour out your heart to those who come running to you longing to know me. I will show you how much love I hold in my heart for all my dear ones. I want to bless you for your faithfulness and trust in me. Receive all that I send you in the way of love and comfort from those I place in your midst. You do not always have to be strong. Let me be strong for you. Your strength in me will in turn give you the rest you desire. The peace that you long for will envelop your heart and soul every day as you rest in me. Bring all your concerns to me and I will break every area of bondage and every stronghold that tries to get in the way of the blessed life that I hold in my hand just for you. I am your Mighty Savior, and you are my precious child of resiliency. **Hold on to the hope I have given you**, it shall never disappoint.

I will hold onto the hope you have given me

Sweet Jesus, how you long to have me sit in your presence and soak in your majesty. I am wonderful in the sight of my Maker. I have made tremendous strides in my journey to your heart. I am an overcomer. With you I am victorious. My life shall bring glory to your name. You care for all my needs, big and small. You are my protector. You are my great provider. No one shall thwart the plans you have for my life for you have called me by name. I am yours. I am chosen. I belong to the Almighty One. Songs of deliverance and freedom are flowing down from the heavens above to rest upon my heart this day. I will receive this music as a sweet comfort to my heart. Joy in great measure you are giving to me, my Jesus. Righteousness and truth is presiding over my heart and mind. Wisdom into the things that are incomprehensible will give me new insight and revelation. I will listen to that still, small voice within my heart that tells me which way to turn at every crossroad in my life. I will pour out my heart to those who come running to me longing to know you. You will show me how much love you hold in your heart for all your dear ones. You want to bless me for my faithfulness and trust in you. I will receive all that you send me in the way of love and comfort from those you place in my midst. I do not always have to be strong. I will let you be strong for me. My strength in you will in turn give me the rest I desire. The peace that I long for will envelop my heart and soul every day as I rest in you. I will bring all my concerns to you and you will break every area of bondage and every stronghold that tries to get in the way of the blessed life that you hold in your hand just for me. You are my mighty Savior, and I am your precious child of resiliency. **I will hold on to the hope you have given me**, *it shall never disappoint.*

Psalm 71:14
**As for me, I will always have hope; I will praise you
more and more.**

38. You can confidently trust that I am always there

Dearest child, I am with you and I am in you. Your heart is aligned to mine. In seeking my face you will come to know deeper truths into the mysteries of my ways. I am the way, the truth and the life. All that I have I give to you in abundance. Quietly come before me and share your deepest thoughts. I will meet you there always. Although you may not always hear me or feel me, **you can confidently trust that I am always there**. I will never leave you nor forsake you. I know the concerns that weigh upon your heart. I have heard the cries of your heart and know the things which are holding you down. Come to me and I will lift your burdens and realign your thoughts with mine. I will give you wisdom that will lead you to truth that brings freedom. You are free in me, my child. I will keep you with me always. In your darkest moments you are never alone. Rest in me and enjoy your day. I will bring new things your way that will bring a smile to your face.

I can confidently trust that you are always there

*Dearest Jesus, you are with me and you are in me. My heart is aligned to yours. In seeking your face I will come to know deeper truths into the mysteries of your ways. You are the way, the truth and the life. All that you have you give to me in abundance. I will quietly come before you and share my deepest thoughts. You will meet me there always. Although I may not always hear you or feel you, **I can confidently trust that you are always there**. You will never leave me nor forsake me. You know the concerns that weigh upon my heart. You have heard the cries of my heart and know the things which are holding me down. I will come to you and you will lift my burdens and realign my thoughts with yours. You will give me wisdom that will lead me to truth that brings freedom. I am free in you, my Jesus. You will keep me with you always. In my darkest moments I am never alone. I will rest in you and enjoy my day. You will bring new things my way that will bring a smile to my face.*

Matthew 28:19-20
Therefore go and make disciples of all nations, baptizing them in the name of the Father and of the Son and of the

*Holy Spirit, and teaching them to obey everything
I have commanded you. And surely I am with you always,
to the very end of the age.*

39. I will continue to reveal myself to you

Dearest child, you are beloved of my heart. Today I stand at the door of your heart and knock. It is a new day to revel in the goodness I have surrounded you with. Take the time today to reflect on all that I am doing in your life, on all the blessings big and small. It is with great joy that I look upon you. I have filled you with love and compassion. I am a shield about you. I am your everlasting joy. I am the one who takes you by the hand and leads the inspirations of your heart. I bring you into a new place with me each and every day. Yes, your days will hold challenges, but that is why I am here for you to lean on. What pleases my heart is your honesty in revealing your heart and thoughts to me. You share it all. The more honest you are with me, the more honest you are becoming with yourself. That is how you grow and mature in your faith. Continue to reveal yourself to me and **I will continue to reveal myself to you**. I do not withhold my love from you. My love is constant. I am your constant companion.

You will continue to reveal yourself to me

*Dearest Jesus, I am beloved of your heart. Today you stand at the door of my heart and knock. It is a new day to revel in the goodness you have surrounded me with. I will take the time today to reflect on all that you are doing in my life, on all the blessings big and small. It is with great joy that you look upon me. You have filled me with love and compassion. You are a shield about me. You are my everlasting joy. You are the one who takes me by the hand and leads the inspirations of my heart. You bring me into a new place with you each and every day. Yes, my days will hold challenges, but that is why you are here for me to lean on. What pleases your heart is my honesty in revealing my heart and thoughts to you. I share it all. The more honest I am with you, the more honest I am becoming with myself. That is how I grow and mature in my faith. I will continue to reveal myself to you and **you will continue to reveal yourself to me**. You do not withhold your love from me. Your love is constant. You are my constant companion.*

Deuteronomy 29:29

The secret things belong to the Lord our God, but the things revealed belong to us and to our children forever, that we may follow all the words of this law.

40. I am your greatest and truest friend

Sweet and tender heart, you are delicate yet strong. The fire of my love burns within you shedding new light and life to those I place around you. When your heart is feeling fragile, I will be the packaging that keeps you from breaking. I will provide layers of protection over your heart and mind. My very Word is your strength, your amour. Remember who you are in me. Remember all the promises I speak of in My Word. Call forth things that are not as though they are in accord with my Word. My Word is your truth. My Word is your covering. My Word is life. Be not weary when the enemy strategizes against you using your very friends to cause you woe. The enemy is always going to try to hit you where it hurts the most. Friendships can bring strength and friendships can bring you down when hearts are not aligned to my will. Remember though, that **I am your greatest and truest friend** and I will never let you down. When you listen to my counsel you will rise above the pettiness and walk in peace. I am your peace. I am your resting place. Rest in me and no matter how hard the enemy hits you, even in your blind spots, I will be the truth that sets you free. Do for others as you would want them to do for you. In doing this, my peace will rest upon you.

You are my greatest and truest friend

*Sweet and tender Jesus, I am delicate yet strong. The fire of your love burns within me shedding new light and life to those you place around me. When my heart is feeling fragile, you will be the packaging that keeps me from breaking. You will provide layers of protection over my heart and mind. Your very Word is my strength, my amour. I will remember who I am in you. I will remember all the promises you speak of in your Word. I will call forth things that are not as though they are in accord with your Word. Your Word is my truth. Your Word is my covering. Your Word is life. I will not be not weary when the enemy strategizes against me using my very friends to cause me woe. The enemy is always going to try to hit me where it hurts the most. Friendships can bring strength and friendships can bring me down when hearts are not aligned to your will. I will remember though, that **you are my greatest and truest friend** and you will never let me down. When I listen to your counsel, I will rise above the pettiness and walk in peace. You are my peace. You are my* *resting place. I will rest in you and no matter how hard the enemy hits me, even in my blind spots, you will be the truth that sets me free. I will do for others as I would want them to do for me. In doing this, your peace will rest upon me.*

Isaiah 41:8-9

But you, Israel, my servant, Jacob, whom I have chosen,

you descendants of Abraham my friend,

I took you from the ends of the earth,

from its farthest corners I called you.

I said, 'You are my servant';

I have chosen you and have not rejected you.

41. I am all the strength you need

I want you to know that whenever the task before you seems too daunting, it is before you for a reason. I want to show you how strong you have become. You may think you are weak, but you are indeed strong for I am within you and I am strong. **I am all the strength you need.** Call upon my name within your heart and mind and I will come running to you. Whenever the day looks bleak and the rain is pouring down, know that I am here to bring rays of sunshine into your heart. Even on the grayest of days, my light is shining ~ the light that warms your heart and refreshes your spirit.

You are all the strength I need

*You want me to know that whenever the task before me seems too daunting, it is before me for a reason. You want to show me how strong I have become. I may think I am weak, but I am indeed strong for you are within me and you are strong. **You are all the strength I need.** I will call upon your name within my heart and mind and you will come running to me. Whenever the day looks bleak and the rain is pouring down, I will know that you are here to bring rays* *of sunshine into my heart. Even on the grayest of days, your light is shining ~ the light that warms my heart and refreshes my spirit.*

Philippians 4:13
I can do all things through Christ who strengthens me. (NKJV)

42. There is nothing that is too big for me

There is nothing that is too big for me. There is nothing that is too difficult for me. There is nothing that will get in the way of my plans for your life as long as you continue to seek my face. I will be with you every step of the way.

There is nothing that is too big for you

There is nothing that is too big for you. There is nothing that is too difficult for you. There is nothing that will get in the way of your plans for my life as long as I continue to seek your face. You will be with me every step of the way.

Jeremiah 32:17
Ah, Sovereign Lord, you have made the heavens and the earth by your great power and outstretched arm. Nothing is too hard for you.

43. I became nothing so you could become something

Today is a new day. As you have walked through the fire with me, so shall you walk in the light of the sun with me, clear skies, warm breezes, birds singing. When you have doubt, come to me into my chamber where we can converse. I will share with you the secrets of my Kingdom, words of wisdom that will bring you insight into how to live your life to the fullest day by day. My sacrifice was for you. I gave myself for you. **I became nothing so you could become something.** And as I rose, so shall you. You shall prosper in many new ways, ways unthought-of of by you. I will lead you gently. You will sail with me, my spirit moving you in the direction you should go. Step aside and let me go before you. Let me clear the pathways for you. If you are always seeking, you shall find. If you are always asking, you shall receive. If you are always knocking, I will open doors for you that you never knew could be opened and often times never even knew were there. Remember, my love for you is abundant and limitless. You have come so far and have so much further to go. This new journey will take you where you never thought you could go. I will show you how much

I love you. You will see it in the abundant fruit that is ready for harvest in your life. This is your time. This is your place. This is your new life. Are you ready? Come and follow me.

You became nothing so I could become something

Today is a new day. As I have walked through the fire with you, so shall I walk in the light of the sun with you, clear skies, warm breezes, birds singing. When I have doubt, I will come to you into your chamber where we can converse. You will share with me the secrets of your Kingdom, words of wisdom that will bring me insight into how to live my life to the fullest day by day. Your sacrifice was for me. You gave yourself for me. **You became nothing so I could become something.** *And as you rose, so shall I. I shall prosper in many new ways, ways unthought-of of by me. You will lead me gently. I will sail with you, your spirit moving me in the direction I should go. I will step aside and let you go before me. I will let you clear the pathways for me. If I am always seeking, I shall find. If I am always asking, I shall receive. If I am always knocking, you will open doors for me that I never knew could be opened and often times never even knew were there. I will remember your love for me is abundant and limitless. I have come so far and have so much further to go. This new journey will take me where I never thought I could* *go. You will show me how much you love me. I will see it in the abundant fruit that is ready for harvest in my life. This is my time. This is my place. This is my new life. I am ready. I will come and follow you.*

2 Timothy 2:11

Here is a trustworthy saying: If we died with him, we will also live with him

44. My Word alone will break through walls

Beloved of my heart, you are shining like a diamond in my Kingdom. Your prayers resonate in the heavens and are gathered unto my heart. As I look upon you, my heart smiles for I am proud of you. I am proud of the way you so earnestly cry out to me and reverently give me praise and honor. Be of good cheer for your Savior is with you to the very end and beyond. I am with you always. As you come up against a wall, take my Word and proclaim its truths. **My Word alone will break through walls**. My Words uttered through the lips of my righteous and obedient servants have a cascading effect in this world ~ they reach abroad, far and wide. I am bringing you to a new level, a higher level, a place where I will share with you new and intimate truths about who I am and who you are to me. I am proud of you. I am with you. I love you.

Your Word alone will break through walls

Jesus of my heart, I am shining like a diamond in your Kingdom. My prayers resonate in the heavens and are gathered unto your heart. As you look upon me, your heart smiles for you are proud of me. You are proud of the way I so earnestly cry out to you and reverently give you praise and honor. I will be of good cheer for my Savior is with me to the very end and beyond. You are with me always. As I come up against a wall, I will take your Word and proclaim its truths. **Your Word alone will break through walls**. Your Word uttered through the lips of your righteous and obedient servants have a cascading effect in this world ~ they reach abroad, far and wide. You are bringing me to a new level, a higher level, a place where you will share with me new and intimate truths about who you are and who I am to you. You are proud of me. You are with me. You love me.

John 17:17

Sanctify them by the truth; your word is truth.

45. I am the one that carries you through the storm

I am the one that carries you through the storm. I am the one that picks you up where you have fallen, holds you, comforts you, restores your confidence and sends you on your way again ~ this time with a better plan for a more fulfilling journey. When you get stuck in a snare set by the enemy, know this ~ you are never stuck for I am Lord of all. As you abandon your own will and submit to me, my spirit is able to penetrate your heart at a deeper level. That is when I unravel thoughts that have collided with fear of the unknown. Remember, I know all and see where you have been, where you are, and where you are heading. If I see that you are leaning in the wrong direction, as a loving parent, I have many ways of leading you back to the path I have set before you. Sometimes it is through discipline which can be painful, but not the kind of pain that disables ~ the kind of pain that enables and causes you to grown and learn. Be encouraged, for I am with you and for you.

You are the one that carries me through the storm

You are the one that carries me through the storm. You are the one that picks me up where I have fallen, holds me, comforts me, restores my confidence and sends me on my way again ~ this time with a better plan for a more fulfilling journey. When I get stuck in a snare set by the enemy, I will know this ~ I am never stuck for you are Lord of all. As I abandon my own will and submit to you, your spirit is able to penetrate my heart at a deeper level. That is when you unravel thoughts that have collided with fear of the unknown. I will remember, you know all and see where I have been, where I am, and where I am heading. If you see that I am leaning in the wrong direction, as a loving parent, you have many ways of leading me back to the path you have set before me. Sometimes it is through discipline which can be painful, but not the kind of pain that disables ~ the kind of pain that enables and causes me to grown and learn. I will be encouraged, for you are with me and for me.

Luke 8:24
The disciples went and woke him, saying, "Master, Master, we're going to drown!" He got up and rebuked the wind and the raging waters; the storm subsided, and all was calm.

127

46. Set aside some time this day to draw near me

Dearest child, you are a joy to my heart. I am thrilled when you experience the kind of joy that comes from me, for it is the truest form of joy. As you revel in all that I am doing in your life, your heart shall be uplifted for you shall see that I am God and I do follow through with my promises spoken of in my Word ~ at all times, in every occasion. My truth is everlasting. My promises are for you ~ to guide you, to lead you down unchartered territories within your heart. My dear child, you must know that as your loving Father, I want the very best for you. What I have to offer has no limits for I am limitless and things that may seem impossible or improbable to you are possible through me and in me. **Set aside some time this day to draw near to me** ~ a moment of stillness where your thoughts rest in me and I will speak to you. In this quiet moment, I will refresh you and let you know that I am with you and I am proud of you. Thank you for taking the time to be with me, it is my greatest pleasure. Where your treasure is there will be your heart. You are my treasure and my heart is with you always!

I will set aside some time this day to draw near you

*Dearest Father, I am a joy to your heart. You are thrilled when I experience the kind of joy that comes from you, for it is the truest form of joy. As I revel in all that you are doing in my life, my heart shall be uplifted for I shall see that you are God and you do follow through with your promises spoken of in your Word ~ at all times, in every occasion. Your truth is everlasting. Your promises are for me ~ to guide me, to lead me down unchartered territories within my heart. My dear Father, I must know that as my loving Father, you want the very best for me. What you have to offer has no limits for you are limitless and things that may seem impossible or improbable to me are possible through you and in you. **I will set aside some time this day to draw near to you** ~ a moment of stillness where my thoughts rest in you and you will speak to me. In this quiet moment, you will refresh me and let me know that you are with me and you are proud of me. You thank me for taking the time to be with you, it is your greatest pleasure. Where my treasure is there will be my heart. I am your treasure and your heart is with me always!*

Hebrews 10:22

Let us draw near to God with a sincere heart and with the full assurance that faith brings, having our hearts sprinkled to cleanse us from a guilty conscience and having our bodies washed with pure water.

47. Jesus, you are my truest friend

Tonight as I lay upon my bed I look to you. Where does my comfort come from? It comes from you, my God. **Jesus, you are my truest friend**. *As I walk through my day I whisper your name at every crossroad and you direct my path. In your mysterious ways you guide my thoughts. Your very name uttered by my lips is a shield about me. Even when I am unsure about how the events of the day are going to unfold, your gentle voice within my heart and mind says all will be well. I believe you.*

Deuteronomy 7:9
Know therefore that the Lord your God is God;
he is the faithful God, keeping his covenant of love
to a thousand generations of those who love him
and keep his commandments.

48. I am building a new strength of character within you

My loving, precious child, I know that you are seeking comfort and hope in areas that have brought you dismay and discord. Help is on the way, dear one. I am here to stand by your side and stand strong on your behalf. When you sink into the depths of despair you are never alone though it may seem as though you are. In the darkness I will shine a light. In the darkness, I will penetrate those areas that need healing with the salve from heaven that my Father used to bind up my wounds. Remember that before I was brought into the house of my Father, I was plunged into the pits of hell, all so I could rise up and defeat the world's enemy. The enemy would love (if it were possible for him to love) for you to fall into the pits of darkness and keep you there bound up. But that is impossible, for I will never let my children go, and you are my most beloved child. As you have followed after me, you have been persecuted for my namesake and have followed in my footsteps. My footsteps take you on the narrow path, but this path leads to life. You are in the process of completely dying to yourself so that you may rise completely to a new life in me. As the parts of you that you have held on to for so many years are being unbound by me, your wounds are being exposed. These wounds need exposure to my light in order to heal properly. If they are kept bound up you will not be able to realize the specific areas that need to be exposed to my light. The deeper you fall, the higher you will rise up. I would have it that you rise up to the very top, so that you have entrance into a special sanctuary in my Father's house that is set apart for those who have persevered. **I am building a new strength of character within you**. All battles come to an end, my dearest child. The one you are currently in is drawing near its end and I have sent my warrior angels to guard and protect you so that you do not stumble. Be brave, my child. Be courageous. Be still before me. Always remember that I am God.

You are building a new strength of character within me

My loving, precious Jesus, you know that I am seeking comfort and hope in areas that have brought me dismay and discord. Help is on the way, my Jesus. You are here to stand by my side and stand strong on my behalf. When I sink into the depths of despair I am never alone though it may seem *as though I am. In the darkness you will shine a light. In the darkness, you will penetrate those areas that need healing with the salve from heaven that your Father used to bind up your wounds. I will remember that before you were brought into the house of your Father, you were plunged into the pits of hell, all so you could rise up and defeat the world's enemy. The enemy would love (if it were possible for him to love) for me to fall into the pits of darkness and keep me there bound up. But that is impossible, for you will never let your children go, and I am your most beloved child. As I have followed after you, I have been persecuted for your name-sake and have followed in your footsteps. Your footsteps take me on the narrow path, but this path leads to life. I am in the process of completely dying to myself so that I may rise completely to a new life in you. As the parts of me that I have held on to for so many years are being unbound by you, my wounds are being exposed. These wounds need exposure to your light in order to heal properly. If they are kept bound up I will not be able to realize the specific areas that need to be exposed to your light. The deeper I fall, the higher I will rise up. You would have it that I rise up to the very top, so that I have entrance into a special sanctuary in your Father's house that is set apart for those who have persevered. **You*** *are building a new strength of character within me. All battles come to an end, my dearest Jesus. The one I am currently in is drawing near its end and you have sent your warrior angels to guard and protect me so that I do not stumble. I will be brave, my Jesus. I will be courageous. I will be still before you. I will always remember that you are God.*

Isaiah 12:2
Surely God is my salvation; I will trust and not be afraid. The Lord, the Lord himself, is my strength and my defense; he has become my salvation."

49. I forgive you

Dearest child, do you know that you are forgiven completely when you come to me asking for forgiveness? Do you really believe that you are? I have washed you as white as snow. I have cleaned the slate so that you may begin again fresh and renewed. Why do I forgive you? The answer is simple ~ because I love you. I created you to be who you are this day. As you walk through your days with everything that a day holds, you are bound to fall because you are human. But you are destined to rise up again as I have first risen for you. Do not be ashamed to come to me for there is nothing to hide. I already know what you are going through in your thoughts, your actions, and in your heart. By coming to me for mercy and acceptance, you will find that I am indeed merciful and fully accept you in every way. Baring your heart and acknowledging your sin before me opens up a window in your heart where the sin flows out and a renewed spirit flows in. Sometimes it is difficult to face your own sin but you do not have to do it alone. I am always here as your friend ready to listen and receive, wash, and redeem. Do I forgive you? Yes. I always will as you seek my face and turn your heart toward righteousness. Be confident in this truth. **I forgive you**.

You forgive me

Dearest Jesus, I know that I am forgiven completely when I come to you asking for forgiveness? I really believe that I am. You have washed me as white as snow. You have cleaned the slate so that I may begin again fresh and renewed. Why do you forgive me? The answer is simple ~ because you love me. You created me to be who I am this day. As I walk through my days with everything that a day holds, I am bound to fall because I am human. But I am destined to rise up again as you have first risen for me. I will not be ashamed to come to you for there is nothing to hide. You already know what I am going through in my thoughts, my actions, and in my heart. By coming to you for mercy and acceptance, I will find that you are indeed merciful and fully accept me in every way. Baring my heart and acknowledging my sin before you opens up a window in my heart where the sin flows out and a renewed spirit flows in. Sometimes it is difficult to face my own sin but I do not have to do it alone. You are always here as my friend ready to listen and receive, wash, and redeem.

Do you forgive me? Yes. You always will as I seek your face and turn my heart toward righteousness. I will be confident in this truth. You forgive me.

Psalm 32:5

Then I acknowledged my sin to you and did not cover up my iniquity. I said, "I will confess my transgressions to the Lord." And you forgave the guilt of my sin.

50. My love for you is constant

I want you to know that I love you. I want you to know that I am proud of you. I want you to know that I consider you worthy, worthy of all my love, of all I have to give my precious children. You are my precious child. When you lack confidence in who I created you to be, come to me in my Word and I will shower you with my promises and my loving kindness. When you feel void of my presence, lift up your heart to mine and I will embrace you with arms wide open. I will show you in many different ways how much I love you and how you are such a treasure to my heart. Be encouraged and know that I am leading you down the right path. There is so much joy that I am sending your way ~ joy that will break down any walls that have come between our hearts. Once those walls come down, and they will, you will see my divinity in a different light. You will receive clarity in the realm of my spirit that draws you into the shelter of the Most High. In this place of shelter, I will pour over you life giving words of love, grace, and mercy. In this place you will know how much I love you. **My love for you is constant** ~ it remains the same no matter where you are in life. I never leave your side. Remember and know that I want the very best for your life. I see what your heart is striving after and I am here to take you to that next level. Exceeding joy is awaiting you. You are joy to my heart just as you are today! Come away with me in your heart! I am waiting for you.

Your love for me is constant

You want me to know that you love me. You want me to know that you are proud of me. You want me to know that you consider me worthy, worthy of all your love, of all you have to give your precious children. I am precious to you, my Jesus. When I lack confidence in who you created me to be, I will come to you in your Word and you will shower me with your promises and your loving kindness. When I feel void of your presence, I will lift up my heart to yours and you will embrace me with arms wide open. You will show me in many different ways how much you love me and how I am such a treasure to your heart. I will be encouraged and know that you are leading me down the right path. There is so much joy that you are sending my way ~ joy that will break down any walls that have come between our hearts. Once those walls come down, and they will, I will see your divinity in a different light. I will receive clarity in the realm of your spirit that draws me into the shelter of the Most High. In this place of shelter, you will pour over me life giving words of love, grace, and mercy. In this place I will know how much you love me. **Your love for me is constant** *~ it remains the same no matter where I am in life. You never leave my side. I will remember and know that you want the very best for my life. You see what my heart is striving after and you are here to take me to that next level. Exceeding joy is awaiting me. I am joy to your heart just as I am today! I will come away with you in my heart! You are waiting for me.*

Psalm 103:17

But from everlasting to everlasting the Lord's love is with those who fear him, and his righteousness with their children's children.

51. You are the apple of my eye

You will see all around you that there are people that need to hear an encouraging word. My children want to feel special. You are special to me and that is what matters the most. **You are the apple of my eye.** It does not matter what other people think about you. What matters is what I think about you. I want you to know this day that I think the world of you just this very moment. I am proud of you. I cherish you.

I am the apple of your eye

*I see all around me that there are people that need to hear an encouraging word. Your children want to feel special. I am special to you and that is what matters the most. **I am the apple of your eye.** It does not matter what other people think about me. What matters is what you think about me. You want me to know this day that you think the world of me just this very moment. You are proud of me. You cherish me.*

Psalm 17:8
Keep me as the apple of your eye; hide me in the shadow of your wings.

52. I have gone before you to make your path straight

Today as you set about your journey, remember to give all your thoughts and cares to me. I will show you the way to go. At every turn my hand is there to guide you. **I have gone before you to make your path straight**.

You have gone before me to make my path straight

Today as I set about my journey, I will remember to give all my thoughts and cares to you. You will show me the way to go. At every turn your hand is there to guide me. You have gone before me to make my path straight.

Proverbs 3:5-7
Trust in the Lord with all your heart and lean not on your own understanding; in all your ways submit to him, and he will make your paths straight.

53. I am walking right by your side

Dearest one, my heart goes out to you this day. In these moments of sadness, loneliness and despair, know this ~ I will never let you go. You are precious to my eyes. Just as you have laid your heart bare before me, so do I open up my heart completely to you. Rest in the comfort of my heart which is steadfast and true. I will make a way for you in the desert. I will lead you down the path that will bring you renewed strength, life, and hope. I want you to know that your best years are yet to come. Continue to hold tight to me. Delight in me and I will give you the desires of your heart. You have walked a lonely road at times but I have always walked down that road with you even when you were not aware that I was there. It is that way this day. **I am walking right by your side**. Be comforted. I delight in you. All will be well.

You are walking right by my side

Dearest Father, your heart goes out to me this day. In these moments of sadness, loneliness and despair, I know this ~ you will never let me go. I am precious to your eyes.

144

Just as I have laid my heart bare before you, so do you open up your heart completely to me. I will rest in the comfort of your heart which is steadfast and true. You will make a way for me in the desert. You will lead me down the path that will bring me renewed strength, life, and hope. You want me to know that my best years are yet to come. I will continue to hold tight to you. I will delight in you and you will give me the desires of my heart. I have walked a lonely road at times but you have always walked down that road with me even when I was not aware that you were there. It is that way this day. **You are walking right by my side.** *I will be comforted. You delight in me. All will be well.*

Psalm 23:4

Even though I walk through the darkest valley, I will fear no evil, for you are with me; your rod and your staff, they comfort me.

54. Let go of the burdens you are carrying

Oh tender heart, do not be dismayed for I am your God. Yes, I will strengthen you and help you and hold you close as you walk down this burdensome path. This day will break forth to a new day. A new day is a new opportunity to make the best of even the most difficult circumstances. I am right by your side. **Let go of all the burdens you are carrying**. Give it all to me. Allow me to lighten your load. I am here for you. I am as close to you as you are to yourself. I am in your heart and know that you are longing for comfort. Be not weary. Be not sad. I want you to know that no matter what you are going through, I have come so that you may find rest. Allow the rivers of my living water to cleanse your heart and renew your mind. I am doing a great work within your heart even amidst your pain. Not one tear goes unnoticed by me. Not one sigh is unheard by me. Not one cry escapes my ears. I hear you. I love you. I know what you need and I am here this day to bring you one step closer to my heart. I have come so that you may find joy again. It is coming. This I promise you.

I will let go of the burdens I am carrying

Oh Father, I will not be dismayed for you are my God. Yes, you will strengthen me and help me and hold me close as I walk down this burdensome path. This day will break forth to a new day. A new day is a new opportunity to make the best of even the most difficult circumstances. You are right by my side. ***I will let go of all the burdens I am carrying.*** *I will give it all to you. I will allow you to lighten my load. You are here for me. You are as close to me as I am to myself. You are in my heart and know that I am longing for comfort. I will not be weary. I will not be sad. You want me to know that no matter what I am going through, you have come so that I may find rest. I will allow the rivers of your living water to cleanse my heart and renew my mind. You are doing a great work within my heart even amidst my pain. Not one tear goes unnoticed by you. Not one sigh is unheard by you. Not one cry escapes your ears. You hear me. You love me. You know what I need and you are here this day to bring me one step closer to your heart. You have come so that I may find joy again. It is coming. This you promise me.*

Matthew 11:30

For my yoke is easy and my burden is light.

147

55. Draw near to me

Dearest child, I am with you now even to the end of the ages. Surrounding you are choirs of angels singing praises along with you unto me in the heavens. In your moments of worship and praise, I am in your midst in a special way. I minister to your heart as you pour out your heart and soul in song to your Maker. I am the one that brings good tidings and I am here to tell you that you are a winner. You have risen to the next level and I am ready to show you who I am and what I am all about. I am in your heart whispering your name. **Draw near to me**, for within my heart is a treasure for you to behold. I give unto you my heart! Rejoice, for a new day is dawning and within this day I will bless you in many ways. Believe in the power of my transforming love and you will see me work wonders in your life. Be at peace this day, for I am right by your side.

I will draw near to you

Dearest Jesus, you are with me now even to the end of the ages. Surrounding me are choirs of angels singing praises along with me unto you in the heavens. In my moments of *worship and praise, you are in my midst in a special way. You minister to my heart as I pour out my heart and soul in song to my Maker. You are the one that brings good tidings and you are here to tell me that I am a winner. I have risen to the next level and you are ready to show me who you are and what you are all about. You are in my heart whispering my name. **I will draw near you,** for within your heart is a treasure for me to behold. You give unto me your heart! I will rejoice, for a new day is dawning and within this day you will bless me in many ways. I will believe in the power of your transforming love and I will see you work wonders in my life. I will be at peace this day, for you are right by my side.*

Psalm 73:28
But it is good for me to draw near to God;
I have put my trust in the Lord God,
that I may declare all your works. (NKJV)

56. Hope in victory

As you call upon my name I come running to you. I hear your every thought. Your heart's cry reaches the throne room of my Father. Yes, my child, this is a battle you are in, but do not fear for I am your captain and it is my responsibility to lead you safely to shore. The waters rage about you, but there is still within you the peace that comes from me. As you slip into the dark waters, see that I have sent the Coastguard to rescue you. I have come with many so that you will not drown. Your victory is bigger than yourself. Your victory will empower you to help others that have fallen into the same deep waters. That hope in me is your **hope in victory**. It is that very hope that makes me proud of you. It is that very hope within you that draws me to you. Hope is light, my child. Your hope in me is drawing in my light. Your hope in me is reaching the heavens. I have charged my greatest angels to surround and protect you so that you do not stumble.

I will hope in victory

As I call upon your name you come running to me. You hear my every thought. My heart's cry reaches the throneroom of my Father. Yes, my Jesus, this is a battle I am in, but I will not fear for you are my captain and it is your responsibility to lead me safely to shore. The waters rage about me, but there is still within me the peace that comes from you. As I slip into the dark waters, I will see that you have sent the Coastguard to rescue me. You have come with many so that I will not drown. My victory is bigger than myself. My victory will empower me to help others that have fallen into the same deep waters. That hope in you is my **hope in victory**. It is that very hope that makes you proud of me. It is that very hope within me that draws me to you. Hope is light, my Jesus. My hope in you is drawing in your light. My hope in you is reaching the heavens. You have charged my greatest angels to surround and protect me so that I do not stumble.

1 Corinthians 15:57
But thanks be to God! He gives us the victory
through our Lord Jesus Christ.

57. It is I who am carrying you through

In the midst of your trials I will come along beside you
and carry you through. You do not have to carry your burdens
alone. Allow me to lift them from your shoulders and bring
you to a new place with me. I am the one that will never leave
your side. I am the one that will show you the way to go. I am
the one that will never disappoint you. I know you have been
disappointed many times in your life by others. You have
also experienced the effects of what you may see as failures.
You are not a failure. You are an overcomer. You keep on
going even despite the circumstances you are facing. How
is it that you are able to make it through these rough times?
It is I who am carrying you through. I am breathing my
breath of hope within you. You may not even realize that it
is I who am moving within you to make it through the day.
I want for you to know that even when my children do not
come to me, I still move on their behalf. You do not have to
come to me for me to be with you for I am always with you.
It is the desire of my heart that you come to me because I
want to teach you new things about yourself and life that will
help you grow and mature in your faith. Draw near to me
this day and I will draw near to you. Be content in the little

things. Be thankful for the blessings I send your way. I send you my blessings just because I love you and want you to taste and see my goodness. I look forward to every moment you call upon my name. Go now and walk into this new day with fervor to be a light unto my children and to brighten someone's day. I will give you what you need always.

It is you who are carrying me through

In the midst of my trials you will come along beside me and carry me through. I do not have to carry my burdens alone. I will allow you to lift them from my shoulders and bring me to a new place with you. You are the one that will never leave my side. You are the one that will show me the way to go. You are the one that will never disappoint me. You know I have been disappointed many times in my life by others. I have also experienced the effects of what I may see as failures. I am not a failure. I am an overcomer. I keep on going even despite the circumstances I am facing. How is it that I am able to make it through these rough times? **It is you who are carrying me me through**. *You are breathing your breath of hope within me. I may not even realize that it is you who are moving within me to make it through the day. You* want for me to know that even when your children do not come to you, you still move on their behalf. I do not have to come to you for you to be with me for you are always with me. It is the desire of your heart that I come to you because you want to teach me new things about myself and life that will help me grow and mature in my faith. I will draw near to you this day and you will draw near to me. I will be content in the little things. I will be thankful for the blessings you send my way. You send me your blessings just because you love me and want me to taste and see your goodness. You look forward to every moment I call upon your name. I will go now and walk into this new day with fervor to be a light unto your children and to brighten someone's day. You will give me what I need always.

Psalm 63:8

I cling to you; your right hand upholds me.

58. Not one thought or cry is escaped from my ears

Let your heart be glad this day, for I am here to bring you good tidings, to spread the word to all my children and let you know that I love you beyond compare. There is nothing that is insignificant to me, **not one thought or cry from your heart is escaped from my ears**. I capture all your tears in my hand and release a refreshing rain upon your spirit to bring you comfort. So many times you have cried out to me and have felt that I have not answered you. Oh, my child, I always answer, but my ways are mysterious to you just as my love for you is fathomless. My love will never escape you. It may feel as though I have abandoned you at times or failed to answer your prayers. Please trust that my infinite love is doing a great work in you during these times. The effects of my love are ever reaching to the ends of time and beyond. This is your opportunity to take my hand and walk with me. In your desperate moments, simply trust in me and I will show you the way to my heart. You will never be lost for I am always at your side. I come to rescue you from where you have fallen. I come to lift you up and dust you off and put you back on the right path, the path of righteousness. I am doing a new work in you this day. Reach out to me, take my hand and walk with me. I have much to share with you.

Not one thought or cry is escaped from your ears

*I will let my heart be glad this day, for you are here to bring me good tidings, to spread the word to all your children and let me know that you love me beyond compare. There is nothing that is insignificant to you, **not one thought or cry from my heart is escaped from your ears**. You capture all my tears in your hand and release a refreshing rain upon my spirit to bring me comfort. So many times I have cried out to you and have felt that you have not answered me. Oh, my Jesus, you always answer, but your ways are mysterious to me just as your love for me is fathomless. Your love will never escape me. It may feel as though you have abandoned me at times or failed to answer my prayers. I will trust that your infinite love is doing a great work in me during these times. The effects of your love are ever reaching to the ends of time and beyond. This is my opportunity to take your hand and walk with you. In my desperate moments, I will simply trust in you and you will show me the way to your heart. I will never be lost for you are always at my side. You*

*come to rescue me from where I have fallen. You come to lift
me up and dust me off and put me back on the right path, the
path of righteousness. You are doing a new work in me this
day. I will reach out to you, take your hand and walk with
you. You have much to share with me.*

Exodus 22:27

When they cry out to me, I will hear,

for I am compassionate.

59. I will bring you encouragement

Seeker of my heart, come to me so that you may find rest. In moments of quiet with me, you will come to know me in deeper, more intimate ways. I have much to share with you. I want you to rest in the comfort of my loving presence. Let me lift the burden off of your shoulders. Allow my healing rains to wash you, cleanse you and free you from all of your anxieties. When you are discouraged, come to me and **I will bring you encouragement**. When you are exhausted, come to me and I will bring you rest. When you are joyful, come to me and we can rejoice together in all the greatness of my love that pours over you day and night. Not one moment passes when I am not with you. I know what you are going through this day and I am here to let you know that despite the trials, you will be victorious for your King and Savior has gone to battle for you. When you are weak, I am strong. Do not be dismayed for I am with you. Lift up your eyes to me and believe that I love you beyond compare. As you pour out your heart to me, I open the floodgates of heaven upon your life to bring you the peace that passes all understanding. Be of good cheer for it is a new day, a day of blessings for you and for all of my beloved children who are calling upon my name.

You will bring me encouragement

My Jesus, I will come to you so that I may find rest. In moments of quiet with you, I will come to know you in deeper, more intimate ways. You have much to share with me. You want me to rest in the comfort of your loving presence. I will let you lift the burden off of my shoulders. I will allow your healing rains to wash me, cleanse me and free me from all of my anxieties. When I am discouraged, I will come to you and **you will bring me encouragement**. *When I am exhausted, I will come to you and you will bring me rest. When I am joyful, I will come to you and we can rejoice together in all the greatness of your love that pours over me day and night. Not one moment passes when you are not with me. You know what I am going through this day and you are here to let me know that despite the trials, I will be victorious for my King and Savior has gone to battle for me. When I am weak, you are strong. I will not be dismayed for you are with me. I will lift up my eyes to you and believe that you love me beyond compare. As I pour out my heart to you, you open* *the floodgates of heaven upon my life to bring me the peace that passes all understanding. I will be of good cheer for it is a new day, a day of blessings for me and for all of your beloved children who are calling upon your name.*

James 4:10

Humble yourselves before the Lord,

and he will lift you up.

60. I will bring you comfort

My sweet child, I am with you. I travel right by your side everywhere you go. I never leave your side. I send my guardian angels to watch over you day and night. Release all your fears to me and **I will bring you comfort**. My peace rests upon you this hour. I want for you to remember that you are never outside of my love.

You will bring me comfort

*My sweet Jesus, you are with me. You travel right by my side everywhere I go. You never leave my side. You send your guardian angels to watch over me day and night. I will release all my fears to you and **you will bring me comfort**. Your peace rests upon me this hour. You want for me to remember that I am never outside of your love.*

Psalm 119:76
May your unfailing love be my comfort, according to your promise to your servant.

61. I have come to fill you with joy

In the darkness of the world that is filled with angry, hurting people ~ my light is within you to bring joy to others. At times you may feel as though there is no joy in your heart. That is alright, for **I have come to fill you with joy** as you walk with me. Your joy can come through the simple gift of hope I give to you this day. Keep hope alive within your heart. Remember to think on good things. I am good and my goodness is for you and in you.

You have come to fill me with joy

In the darkness of the world that is filled with angry, hurting people ~ your light is within me to bring joy to others. At times I may feel as though there is no joy in my heart. That is alright, for ***you have come to fill me with joy*** *as I walk with you. My joy can come from the simple gift of hope you give to me this day. I will keep hope alive within my heart. I will remember to think on good things. You are good and your goodness is for me and in me.*

Psalm 19:8

The precepts of the Lord are right, giving joy to the heart.

The commands of the Lord are radiant, giving light to the eyes.

62. Jesus, you are my inspiration

Oh Lord, you are always by my side. Never once have you abandoned me. Your love keeps me safe and brings me comfort. How is it that you do what you do? That I do not know, but what I do know is that you are awesome, you are magnificent, you are amazing! **Jesus, you are my inspiration.** *Your plans for my life far supersede what I could imagine for myself. Yes, each day holds its own challenges, but it is in overcoming these challenges that I see the strength you have birthed within me because I continue to trust in you. My confidence is in you and comes through you.*

Ephesians 3:19-21 (NKJV)
Now to Him who is able to do exceedingly abundantly above all that we ask or think, according to the power that works in us, to Him be glory in the church by Christ Jesus to all generations, forever and ever. Amen.

63. You have been fearfully and wonderfully made

I am making a way for you in this world. I go before you to make your path straight. As you journey down the trail of life, remember that you are not walking alone. Sometimes you may feel alone. Sometimes you may feel as though you have lost your way. You are not lost because you are not alone – I am with you. I have the directions with me that will lead you to a better place. Stand up and proclaim the truth of my Word and in doing so you will be opening doors that may have been locked to you in the past. I have the keys. Come home, my beloved – come and sit at my banquet table and let me share with you how much I love you. Let me pour over you life giving words of encouragement and hope to brighten your day. I don't think you realize how wonderful you are to me. **You have been fearfully and wonderfully made** by your Creator, out of my undying love for you. Take some time this day to reflect on my goodness – to reflect on my majesty, to reflect on the greatness of your God – your God who sent his very own beloved Son to die for you, to wash away your sins and to raise you up to a new life with me. Enjoy your day and know that you are the work of my hand and are my priceless masterpiece. I have called you today to be with me. I await your arrival and am here to tell you – I love you.

I have been fearfully and wonderfully made

*You are making a way for me in this world. You go before me to make my path straight. As I journey down the trail of life, I will remember that I am not walking alone. Sometimes I feel alone. Sometimes I feel as though I have lost my way. I am not lost because I am not alone – you are with me. You have the directions with you that will lead me to a better place. I will stand up and proclaim the truth of your Word and in doing so you will be opening doors that may have been locked to me in the past. You have the keys. I will come, Jesus, and sit at your banquet table and let you share with me how much you love me. I will let you pour over me life giving words of encouragement and hope to brighten my day. I am wonderful to you. **I have been fearfully and wonderfully made** by my Creator, out of your undying love for me. I will take some time this day to reflect on your goodness – to reflect on your majesty, to reflect on the greatness of my God – my God who sent His very own* *beloved Son to die for me, to wash away my sins and to raise me up to a new life with Him. I will enjoy my day and know that I am the work of your hand and I am your priceless masterpiece. You have called me today to be with you. You await my arrival and are here to tell me – you love me.*

Psalm 139:4

I praise you because I am fearfully and wonderfully made; your works are wonderful, I know that full well.

64. I have heard the cry of your heart

Precious child, I want you to lift up your heart to me in prayer tonight. I have much to share with you. The road you have traveled has been long and arduous but rest assured it has been worth the fight to receive the prize for which you have battled. Your suffering has brought you to your knees before me countless times. **I have heard every cry of your heart.** I have captured every whisper of love you have poured out of your heart and soul to me. Your love of me has been your transformational grace that is molding you into the person I created you to be. Come, my child, to the banquet table and feast with me, your beloved Savior. I will shower you now with love that you have never received before ~ new love that is coming from my throne room in heaven. Savor every moment we share with one another. You belong to me, precious heart. I will take good care of you always. I am overflowing with love for you. I am well pleased with you. Take my hand and walk with me. I will never let you down.

You have heard the cry of my heart

*Precious Jesus, you want me to lift up my heart to you in prayer tonight. You have much to share with me. The road I have traveled has been long and arduous but I will rest assured it has been worth the fight to receive the prize for which I have battled. My suffering has brought me to my knees before you countless times. **You have heard every cry of my heart**. You have captured every whisper of love I have poured out of my heart and soul to you. My love of you has been my transformational grace that is molding me into the person you created me to be. I will come, my Jesus, to the banquet table and feast with you, my beloved Savior. You will shower me now with love that I have never received before ~ new love that is coming from your throne room in heaven. I will savor every moment we share with one another. I belong to you, precious Jesus. You will take good care of me always. You are overflowing with love for me. You are well pleased with me. I will take your hand and walk with you. You will never let me down.*

Psalm 18:6

In my distress I called to the Lord; I cried to my God for help. From his temple he heard my voice; my cry came before him, into his ears.

65. It is for my glory

It is for my glory that you have risen to new life. It is for my glory that you are victorious. It is for my glory that your testimony will bring hope to my children who are calling out to me. You have been set free, my child. This is your new season. This is the season of the great harvest. You will now reap what you have sown. You have sown your love in me and in return I will give unto you one hundred fold. You cannot even imagine what I have in store for your life. You will no longer remain stagnant. You will now soar to new heights on eagles wings. My winds of righteousness will carry you to places you have never been. Your years of hardship will be a distant memory to you. You have much to look forward to. Continue spending time with me and I will pour out upon you great wisdom, understanding and knowledge. A new day for you to shine like never before has arrived just in time for my glory to be revealed in you and through you. Go forth and enjoy this new season. Rejoice in me as I rejoice in you. It is your day to shine. You are shining for my glory which is upon you now and forever more!

It is for your glory

It is for your glory *that I have risen to new life. It is for your glory that I am victorious. It is for your glory that my testimony will bring hope to your children who are calling out to you. I have been set free, my Jesus! This is my new season. This is the season of the great harvest. I will now reap what I have sown. I have sown my love in you and in return you will give unto me one hundred fold. I cannot even imagine what you have in store for my life. I will no longer remain stagnant. I will now soar to new heights on eagles wings. Your winds of righteousness will carry me to places I have never been. My years of hardship will be a distant memory to me. I have much to look forward to. I will continue spending time with you and you will pour out upon me great wisdom, understanding and knowledge. A new day for me to shine like never before has arrived just in time for your glory to be revealed in me and through me. I will go forth and enjoy this new season. I rejoice in you as you rejoice in me. It is my day to shine. I am shining for your glory which is upon me now and forever more!*

Luke 2:14
Glory to God in the highest heaven, and on earth peace to those on whom his favor rests.

66. I am with you

Oh lovely child, I want for you to know that no matter what you do or where you go, **I am with you**. I have not forgotten you. I hold you near to my heart at all times. This day remember to reflect on my goodness. Think of all the things I have done for you. In doing this, you will be strengthened in your spirit. Perseverance is part of the journey to freedom. Keep on persevering and you will find the freedom you have been longing for. Know this, my child, I have called you to be a warrior, to lead the way, to break through walls and be victorious. Draw your strength from my life giving Word. In my Word you will find all that you need to make it through your day successfully. Be quiet before me and remember that I am God.

You are with me

*Oh Father, you want for me to know that no matter what I do or where I go, **you are with me**. You have not forgotten me. You hold me near to your heart at all times. This day I will remember to reflect on your goodness. I will think of all the things you have done for me. In doing this, I will* *be strengthened in my spirit. Perseverance is part of the journey to freedom. I will keep on persevering and I will find the freedom I have been longing for. I know this, Father, you have called me to be a warrior, to lead the way, to break through walls and be victorious. I will draw my strength from your life giving Word. In your Word I will find all that you need to make it through my day successfully. I will be quiet before you and remember that you are God.*

Isaiah 41:10

So do not fear, for I am with you; do not be dismayed, for I am your God. I will strengthen you and help you; I will uphold you with my righteous right hand.

67. I am your Father who loves you

Oh sweet and tender child of mine, how I love you. You are radiant and precious to me. I listen intently to your every prayer. I implore you to keep on seeking and you will find the answers deep within your heart where I reside. Thank you for inviting me in to dwell with you. Thank you for making your heart my home. Even when you do things you are not happy about, I still love you. I understand you and want to teach you the right way, my way. Do not worry anymore about the mistakes and failures of your past. Look forward to the future and remember to always keep your eyes steadfast upon me. **I am your Father who loves you** and wants the very best for you. Take my hand and walk with me. See! I have much to give to you. As the desires of your heart align with my will, they will come to pass in the right time. Be patient. Be still before me and be comforted in my presence. I place a mantle of protection upon you this night. It will never leave you for I am that mantle just as I am your covering. Rest this night in my love. All will be well. Tomorrow is a new beginning for you. I give you a new day as my gift to you. Treasure me as I treasure you. Love me as I love you.

You are my Father who loves me

Oh Father, how you love me. I am radiant and precious to you. You listen intently to my every prayer. You implore me to keep on seeking and I will find the answers deep within my heart where you reside. You thank me for inviting you in to dwell with me. You thank me for making my heart your home. Even when I do things I am not happy about, you still love me. You understand me and want to teach me the right way, your way. I will not worry anymore about the mistakes and failures of my past. I will look forward to the future and remember to always keep my eyes steadfast upon you. **You are my Father who loves me** and wants the very best for me. I will take your hand and walk with you. I will see! You have much to give to me. As the desires of my heart align with your will, they will come to pass in the right time. I will be patient. I will be still before you and be comforted in your presence. You place a mantle of protection upon me this night. It will never leave me for you are that mantle just as you are my covering. I will rest this night in your love. All will be well. Tomorrow is a new beginning for me. You give me a new day as your gift to me. I will treasure you as you treasure me. I will love you as you love me.

1 John 3:1

See what great love the Father has lavished on us,

that we should be called children of God!

And that is what we are! The reason the world does not

know us is that it did not know him.

68. I am intently listening

I am intently listening to every word that you are sharing with me. I understand what you are working through in your heart and I am here to help you. When you are weary come to me so that you can rest. You do not have to figure everything out in one night. Take it piece by piece, step by step. I am accompanying you on this journey so that you do not have to walk it alone. Ask me anything. Tell me everything that is on your heart. Do not fear that I will reject you. I know everything there is to know about you and I love you completely just as you are this moment, imperfections and all. I want you to share it all so that we can sort out your thoughts together and bring them into alignment with my will for your life. There is so much goodness for you to behold in your today and in your tomorrows. There is so much in store for you coming from me out of the treasuries of heaven. I want to show you my love in ways you have yet to experience. Talk to me, my child. I am listening.

You are intently listening

You are intently listening to every word that I am sharing with you. You understand what I am working through in my heart and you are here to help me. When I am weary I will come to you so that I can rest. I do not have to figure everything out in one night. I will take it piece by piece, step by step. You are accompanying me on this journey so that I do not have to walk it alone. I will ask you anything. I will tell you everything that is on my heart. I will not fear that you will reject me. You know everything there is to know about me and you love me completely just as I am this moment, imperfections and all. You want me to share it all so that we can sort out my thoughts together and bring them into alignment with your will for my life. There is so much goodness for me to behold in my today and in my tomorrows. There is so much in store for me coming from you out of the treasuries of heaven. You want to show me your love in ways I have yet to experience. I will talk to you, Jesus. You are listening.

Psalm 17:6
I call on you, my God, for you will answer me; turn your ear to me and hear my prayer.

69. A thankful heart brings me great joy

Dearest child, do not fear, for I am holding onto you this day. Bring all your cares to me and I will shower you with my loving kindness. Continue pressing into me and I will continue to impart my wisdom and truth to you. You will come to understand all that I am doing in your life. Everything has a purpose. All that you go through serves a perfect purpose. It may not seem perfect as you are going through it, but it is all part of the journey I set before you before you were even born. You are making your way through life like a champion. You keep on rising every time you fall. That is the champion spirit I placed within you. Yes, it may seem like I have forsaken you at times. That is far from the truth. As life events unfold, you will be able to look back and see how I have woven your life together as part of a beautiful love song that has no end. Your life is a love song. Sing to me within your heart this day and I will sing back to you. I give you all that I have. I have everything to give and I give it all to you. **A thankful heart brings me great joy**. Today as your heart looks up to me ~ let your heart open up and smile. I have placed a smile in your heart. My beloved, you make my heart smile!

A thankful heart brings you great joy

Dearest Father, I will not fear, for you are holding onto me this day. I will bring all my cares to you and you will shower me with your loving kindness. I will continue pressing into you and you will continue to impart your wisdom and truth to me. I will come to understand all that you are doing in my life. Everything has a purpose. All that I go through serves a perfect purpose. It may not seem perfect as I am going through it, but it is all part of the journey you set before me before I was even born. I am making my way through life like a champion. I keep on rising every time I fall. That is the champion spirit you placed within me. Yes, it may seem like you have forsaken me at times. That is far from the truth. As life events unfold, I will be able to look back and see how you have woven my life together as part of a beautiful love song that has no end. My life is a love song. I will sing to you within my heart this day and you will sing back to me. You give you all that you have. You have everything to give and you give it all to me. A thankful heart brings you great joy. Today as my heart looks up to you, I will let my heart open up and smile. You have placed a smile in my heart. My Father, I make your heart smile!

Psalm 9:1

I will give thanks to you, Lord, with all my heart;
I will tell of all your wonderful deeds.

70. Trust in me

My child, I hear the cries of your heart. I know and understand your pain. I am here to wipe the tears that stream down your face as you look to me for answers. There is nothing that is too difficult for me. It may seem too difficult for you but you are not alone. You do not have to carry the load alone. Allow me to lift the weight upon your shoulders and strengthen your spirit. Have hope, my child. Have hope. **Trust in me** and I will continue to keep that hope alive within you. That hope will give you the strength and courage to face the storm and walk through it with confidence. I am taking you by the hand this day and leading you to walk beside still waters. Soak in my love for I give it to you in abundance. I am teaching you many things about yourself on this journey. What I teach you will help you discern the direction you need to take. You are doing well. You may not feel that way but I want you to feel assured that you are indeed doing well simply because you are reaching out to me. In the midst of your circumstances remember to be thankful and that will help you to change your mindset and help keep you on the right course. Believe and hope. I am with you to satisfy the longings of your heart. Be patient, for they are coming just in time.

I will trust in you

*My Jesus, you hear the cries of my heart. You know and understand my pain. You are here to wipe the tears that stream down my face as I look to you for answers. There is nothing that is too difficult for you. It may seem too difficult for me but I am not alone. I do not have to carry the load alone. I will allow you to lift the weight upon my shoulders and strengthen my spirit. I will have hope, my Father. I will have hope. **I will trust in you** and you will continue to keep that hope alive within me. That hope will give me the strength and courage to face the storm and walk through it with confidence. You are taking me by the hand this day and leading me to walk beside still waters. I will soak in your love for you give it to me in abundance. You are teaching me many things about myself on this journey. What you teach me will help me discern the direction I need to take. I am doing well. I may not feel that way but you want me to feel assured that I am indeed doing well simply because I am reaching out to you. In the midst of my circumstances I will remember to* *be thankful and that will help me to change my mindset and help keep me on the right course. I will believe and hope. You are with me to satisfy the longings of my heart. I will be patient, for they are coming just in time.*

Isaiah 12:2
Surely God is my salvation; I will trust and not be afraid. The Lord, the Lord himself, is my strength and my defense; he has become my salvation."

71. I am your strength when you are weak

My beloved child, do not be dismayed for I am with you. I am your strong tower and your shield. I stand with you in the midst of your trials. I am teaching you how to trust in me in deeper ways. Your longings do not go unnoticed by me. I know all the desires of your heart for it is I who placed them there to begin with. I am cultivating your heart, mind, and soul to be a warrior that will stand in the gap for others who are hurting, lost and broken. In the secret places of your heart where we meet each day, I am teaching you new things. It may seem like one day floats into another with no changes. Realize that you are exercising your spiritual muscles every time you come to me exposing your hurts, trusting that I will lift you up to higher places. Your faithfulness is making you stronger and stronger each day. You may not realize how strong you have become. You will recognize your strength in the days to come as you see the answers to your prayers for yourself and others spring to life before your very eyes. Be encouraged and rest in me. Remember this ~ **I am your strength when you are weak**.

You are my strength when I am weak

My beloved Jesus, I will not be dismayed for you are with me. You are my strong tower and my shield. You stand with me in the midst of my trials. You are teaching me how to trust in you in deeper ways. My longings do not go unnoticed by you. You know all the desires of my heart for it is you who placed them there to begin with. You are cultivating my heart, mind, and soul to be a warrior that will stand in the gap for others who are hurting, lost and broken. In the secret places of my heart where we meet each day, you are teaching me new things. It may seem like one day floats into another with no changes. I will realize that I am exercising my spiritual muscles every time I come to you exposing my hurts, trusting that you will lift me up to higher places. My faithfulness is making me stronger and stronger each day. I may not realize how strong I have become. I will recognize my strength in the days to come as I see the answers to my prayers for myself and others spring to life before my very eyes. I will be encouraged and rest in you. I will remember this ~ you are my strength when I am weak.

Isaiah 40:29
He gives strength to the weary and increases
the power of the weak.

72. I am about to do a new thing

My love surrounds you. My compassion carries you through the most difficult days. Be encouraged for **I am about to do a new thing** in your life, something unexpected. The tides do change and so do life circumstances. From deep within your heart I will raise up a new, vibrant and healthy crop of righteousness. The great harvest is at hand so prepare yourself this hour and follow after me. Be kind to those who are good to you and to those who cause you woe. My children who are hurting need a kind word to bring light and hope to their day. Often times those who do not know me are those who are hurting the most. The hurt that they may bring you is a manifestation of the hurt and emptiness they feel inside. I will give you the grace to show my love to these souls as I call my lost sheep into my fold. Be patient and above all, love.

You are about to do a new thing

*Your love surrounds me. Your compassion carries me through the most difficult days. I will be encouraged for **you are about to do a new thing** in my life, something unexpected.*

The tides do change and so do life circumstances. From deep within my heart you will raise up a new, vibrant and healthy crop of righteousness. The great harvest is at hand so I will prepare myself this hour and follow after you. I will be kind to those who are good to me and to those who cause me woe. Your children who are hurting need a kind word to bring light and hope to their day. Often times those who do not know you are those who are hurting the most. The hurt that they may bring me is a manifestation of the hurt and empti-ness they feel inside. You will give me the grace to show your love to these souls as you call your lost sheep into your fold. I will be patient and above all, I will love.

Isaiah 42:9
See, the former things have taken place,
and new things I declare; before they spring into
being I announce them to you."

73. I do have a plan for you

Seek me with all of your heart. Draw near to me and I will draw near to you. Believe in me. Believe that I honor your prayers and answer them in love. Sometimes you are faced with adversity and trials that seem too difficult to bear. I understand the trial you are going through. I am here to help you weather this storm. No matter how hard the wind is blowing or how turbulent the waters are rushing about you ~ I am with you holding you tighter than you can imagine and I will never let you go. Please do not let go of me. This storm will pass even as the pain may linger. You cannot see the end from the beginning as I do. You can only press forward each day and hold onto my promise that I will never leave you nor forsake you even in this dark hour. **I do have a plan for you** though it may not be clear to you now. I will send many your way to gird you up and speak hope into your life. Hope against all hope and I will make a way for you and your family. I have each one of you in the palm of my hand. I am the comfort you need and I give it to you this day in abundance for you have sought after me in this storm and have been faithful to trust in me despite the circumstances you are facing. I will make a way where there seems to be no way. There is beauty that will rise out of the ashes through it all and you will know that I am your God. I look upon you this day with great compassion.

You do have a plan for me

I will seek you with all of my heart. I will draw near to you and you will draw near to me. I will believe in you. I will believe that you honor my prayers and answer them in love. Sometimes I am faced with adversity and trials that seem too difficult to bear. You understand the trial I am going through. You are here to help me weather this storm. No matter how hard the wind is blowing or how turbulent the waters are rushing about me ~ you are with me holding me tighter than I can imagine and you will never let me go. I will not let go of you. This storm will pass even as the pain may linger. I cannot see the end from the beginning as you do. I can only press forward each day and hold onto your promise that you will never leave me nor forsake me even in this dark hour. ***You do have a plan for me*** *though it may not be clear to me now. You will send many my way to gird me up and speak hope into my life. I will hope against all hope and you will make a way for me and my family. You have each one of us* *in the palm of your hand. You are the comfort I need and you give it to me this day in abundance for I have sought after you in this storm and have been faithful to trust in you despite the circumstances I am facing. You will make a way where there seems to be no way. There is beauty that will rise out of the ashes through it all and I will know that you are my God. You look upon me this day with great compassion.*

Jeremiah 29:11
"For I know the plans I have for you," declares the Lord, "plans to prosper you and not to harm you, plans to give you hope and a future."

74. I am preparing you

Walk in my light this day. As you embark upon a new journey, take my hand and let me lead you beside still waters. I look upon you with great admiration for your faithfulness and loyalty to my calling upon your life. Be encouraged and realize that not one prayer or thought toward me goes unnoticed. I have called you to be a warrior in my Kingdom, to fight the battle for goodness through prayer. I take your prayers and bring them before my Father pleading on your behalf and on the behalf of those you are praying for. Many people in your life have brought you sorrows over the years, but be not dismayed for your faithfulness to me as you have guarded yourself from the attacks of the enemy will be counted to you as righteousness. Release those hurts to me and allow my spirit of forgiveness to cleanse your heart, soul and mind so that you may walk before me in purity. **I am preparing you** for the day when I take you before my Father. On that day you will fully realize my redemption and all that took place when I died on the cross for you. You cannot turn back the hands of time, but you can make good and holy choices this day, this moment. Your sins are forgiven the moment you ask for forgiveness. Do not allow the enemy to plague you with your past sins and failures. Move forward. It is indeed a new day to walk in righteousness. I will always help you along the way as you ask of me. I go before you during your day and orchestrate things on your behalf. I am preparing you to become stronger in your faith as will be needed in the days ahead. You are called to be a light unto my children. My light in you shines hope upon the lives of others that you come in contact with each day. You may not realize the impact you have in my Kingdom for simply being you, the you I created you to be. Trust in me that your faithfulness has a great reward. Walk in my light this day as I send you many blessings just because I love you.

You are preparing me

I will walk in your light this day. As I embark upon a new journey, I will take your hand and let you lead me beside still waters. You look upon me with great admiration for my faithfulness and loyalty to your calling upon my life. I will be encouraged and realize that not one prayer or thought toward you goes unnoticed. You have called me to be a warrior in your Kingdom, to fight the battle for goodness through prayer. You take my prayers and bring them before *your Father pleading on my behalf and on the behalf of those I am praying for. Many people in my life have brought me sorrows over the years, but I will not be dismayed for my faithfulness to you as I have guarded myself from the attacks of the enemy will be counted to me as righteousness. I will release those hurts to you and allow your spirit of forgiveness to cleanse my heart, soul and mind so that I may walk before you in purity. **You are preparing me** for the day when you take me before your Father. On that day I will fully realize your redemption and all that took place when you died on the cross for me. I cannot turn back the hands of time, but I can make good and holy choices this day, this moment. My sins are forgiven the moment I ask for forgiveness. I will not allow the enemy to plague me with my past sins and failures. I will move forward. It is indeed a new day to walk in righteousness. You will always help me along the way as I ask of you. You go before me during my day and orchestrate things on my behalf. You are preparing me to become stronger in my faith as will be needed in the days ahead. I am called to be a light unto your children. Your light in me shines hope upon the lives of others that I come in contact with each day. I may not realize the impact I have in your Kingdom for simply being me, the me you created me to be. I will trust* *in you that my faithfulness has a great reward. I will walk in your light this day as you send me many blessings just because you love me.*

John 14:3
***And if I go and prepare a place for you,
I will come back and take you to be with me that
you also may be where I am.***

75. I am calling you to step out of the boat

My child, I understand where you are right now. Trust that I am with you, even though you do not feel my presence. I am teaching you a new thing. **I am calling you to step out of the boat** and stand on the water with me. Do not be afraid for I am with you. Even though you cannot see all that I am doing behind the scenes on your behalf, trust in me. Believe in me and all will be well with your soul. I love you beyond compare. You are a treasure to be hidden no longer. I am here to bring you out into the world under the radiant glow of my light. My light is your covering and protection this day.

You are calling me to step out of the boat

*My Jesus, you understand where I am right now. I will trust that you are with me, even though I do not feel your presence. You are teaching me a new thing. **You are calling me to step out of the boat** and stand on the water with you. I will not be afraid for you are with me. Even though I cannot see all that you are doing behind the scenes on my behalf, I will trust in you. I will believe in you and all will be well* *with my soul. You love me beyond compare. I am a treasure to be hidden no longer. You are here to bring me out into the world under the radiant glow of your light. Your light is my covering and protection this day.*

Matthew 14:29

"Come," he said. Then Peter got down out of the boat, walked on the water and came toward Jesus.

76. As you seek answers, you will find them

My gracious child, I am with you today. When you are in a place of dissatisfaction with your life, be quiet before me and remember that I am God. I am speaking to you on many different levels. I am speaking to your heart, your mind, and your soul. As you are fervently seeking my direction for your life, remember that I am a God that is faithful to answer. I am listening intently to the cries of your heart. When you are unsettled in your spirit, that is a sign that there is a battle going on around you. If you are not able to see it with your eyes, then it is a battle that is being fought in the realm of the Spirit. Take my Word and fight the good fight and you will be victorious. **As you seek answers, you will find them.** There will be days where you will need to just wait on me and be patient. Be patient, my child, be patient. Sing a new song to me this day and I will capture it in my arms. I will pour out on you a new rain that will freshen the air and cleanse your spirit. The sun is shining and the birds are singing. Join them as you praise my name and you will be filled with the fullness of my light!

As I seek answers, I will find them

*My gracious Father, you are with me today. When I am in a place of dissatisfaction with my life, I will be quiet before you and remember that you are God. You are speaking to me on many different levels. You are speaking to my heart, my mind, and my soul. As I am fervently seeking your direction for my life, I will remember that you are a God that is faithful to answer. You are listening intently to the cries of my heart. When I am unsettled in my spirit, that is a sign that there is a battle going on around me. If I am not able to see it with your eyes, then it is a battle that is being fought in the realm of the Spirit. I will take your Word and fight the good fight and I will be victorious. **As I seek answers, I will find them**. There will be days where I will need to just wait on you and be patient. I will be patient, my Father, I will be patient. I will sing a new song to you this day and you will capture it in your arms. You will pour out on me a new rain that will freshen the air and cleanse my spirit. The sun is shining and the birds are singing. I will join them as I praise your name and I will be filled with the fullness of your light!*

Matthew 7:7

Ask and it will be given to you; seek and you will find;
knock and the door will be opened to you.

77. I will go before you and make your path straight

A new day has arrived! Come and take a walk with me! I will refresh your spirit and renew your mind. Before you set out on your day, turn your eyes toward me. I will help you to walk in truth and righteousness. Be right! Do right! Live right! Purpose in your mind to brighten someone's day with a smile. Speak with confidence and enthusiasm as you walk in my joy. Be grateful! Be thankful! Be hopeful! Be joyful! Be full of love! No matter how you are feeling when you begin your day, first acknowledge my presence and pray your day forward. **I will go before you and make your path straight.** I am full of love for you!

You will go before me and make my path straight

A new day has arrived! You will come and take a walk with me! You will refresh my spirit and renew my mind. Before I set out on my day, you will turn your eyes toward me. You will help me to walk in truth and righteousness. I will be right! I will do right! I will live right! I will purpose in my mind to brighten someone's day with a smile. I will speak with confidence and enthusiasm as I walk in your joy. I will be grateful! I will be thankful! I will be hopeful! I will be joyful! I will be full of love! No matter how I am feeling when I begin my day, I will first acknowledge your presence and pray my day forward. **You will go before me and make my path straight.** *You are full of love for me!*

Proverbs 3:6
In all your ways submit to him, and he will make your paths straight.

78. You were born for this

My hand of victory is upon you. You are steeped in my love and overflowing with abundant grace. My majesty rests upon your shoulders to give you all the strength you need to fulfill my greatest purpose for your life. You are coming in on the home stretch. Reach out and take my baton. Win the race and receive your prize that I have held in my hand just for you. All will see my glory. All glory and honor goes to the Father who has given you new life. I am expanding your horizons and enlarging your territories. All deposits of your faith in me are being credited back to you in amazing proportions. Rise to the occasion and pursue your greatest dream. It is I who placed the dream in your heart. **You were born for this**, in this time, this place, this day. Grace is being poured out upon you through my hands and the hands of our Father. Go now and claim your victory. It will be everlasting and true born out of perseverance, faith, and trust in me. I am running with you, setting the pace by which you will have the energy to sprint to the finish line with great speed and agility. This marathon of life that has been an enduring challenge is coming into a new season. I am with you to refresh your spirit. I have equipped you with what you need to call my children to meet me at the finish line. All will see my glory and know that you belong to me, my winning child.

I was born for this

*Your hand of victory is upon me. I am steeped in your love and overflowing with abundant grace. Your majesty rests upon my shoulders to give me all the strength I need to fulfill your greatest purpose for my life. I am coming in on the home stretch. I will reach out and take your baton. I will the race and receive my prize that you have held in your hand just for me. All will see your glory. All glory and honor goes to the Father who has given me new life. You are expanding my horizons and enlarging my territories. All deposits of my faith in you are being credited back to me in amazing proportions. I will rise to the occasion and pursue my greatest dream. It is you who placed the dream in my heart. **I was born for this**, in this time, this place, this day. Grace is being poured out upon me through your hands and the hands of our Father. I will go now and claim my victory. It will be everlasting and true born out of perseverance, faith, and trust in you. You are running with me, setting the pace by which I will have the energy to sprint to the finish line with* *great speed and agility. This marathon of life that has been an enduring challenge is coming into a new season. You are with me to refresh my spirit. You have equipped me with what I need to call your children to meet you at the finish line. All will see your glory and know that I belong to you, my Jesus.*

Exodus 9:16
But I have raised you up for this very purpose,
that I might show you my power and that my name
might be proclaimed in all the earth.

79. This battle has already been won!

When you are downtrodden and struggling with despair and hopelessness, look up. Cast your cares upon me and allow me to be your protection. When facing the giants in your life, come to me first and I will endow your spirit with the finest armory that will protect you from the fiery darts of the enemy. Satan is very crafty and skilled at twisting around your own thoughts, steeping them with negativity and making it seem as though those thoughts are coming from yourself. This is why it is so important for you to call upon my name. My Spirit will make my Word come alive within you so that you can slay those thoughts and put them to rest by replacing them with the Truth. The truth is that you were fearfully and wonderfully made. The truth is that no weapon formed against you will prevail. The truth is that my love for you never fails. Even if you feel as if you are alone in this battle, remember this truth ~ I will never leave you nor forsake you. My truth will send the enemy to flight and set you free. The enemy has no power to stand up against the truth and as you proclaim the truth there is nothing more he can do but flee. **This battle has already been won!**

This battle has already been won!

*When I am downtrodden and struggling with despair and hopelessness, I will look up. I will cast my cares upon you and allow you to be my protection. When facing the giants in my life, I will come to you first and you will endow my spirit with the finest armory that will protect me from the fiery darts of the enemy. Satan is very crafty and skilled at twisting around my own thoughts, steeping them with negativity and making it seem as though those thoughts are coming from myself. This is why it is so important for me to call upon your name. Your Spirit will make your Word come alive within me so that I can slay those thoughts and put them to rest by replacing them with the Truth. The truth is that I was fearfully and wonderfully made. The truth is that no weapon formed against me will prevail. The truth is that your love for me never fails. Even if I feel as if I am alone in this battle, I will remember this truth ~ you will never leave me nor forsake me. Your truth will send the enemy to flight and set me free. The enemy has no power to stand up against the truth and as I proclaim the truth there is nothing more he can do but flee. **This battle has already been won!***

Psalm 20:6

Now this I know: The Lord gives victory to his anointed.

He answers him from his heavenly sanctuary with the

victorious power of his right hand.

80. Rest in my peace

Oh, that you could fathom my love for you! Just open your heart and allow my healing rains to wash you and cleanse you from anything that is getting in the way of your freedom. My love is extending unto you from the heavens above and from deep within your heart where I reside. You are a wonderful treasure to behold. Your heart is so precious to me. Let me capture all of your anxieties and concerns within my hands so that you may experience peace that is unexplainable. The peace I give to you, I give to you in abundance. **Rest in my peace** and all will be well this day.

I will rest in your peace

Oh, that I could fathom your love for me! I will just open my heart and allow your healing rains to wash me and cleanse me from anything that is getting in the way of my freedom. Your love is extending unto you from the heavens above and from deep within my heart where you reside. I am a wonderful treasure to behold. My heart is so precious to you. I will let you capture all of my anxieties and concerns within your hands so that I may experience peace that is *unexplainable. The peace you give to me, you give to me in abundance. **I will rest in your peace** and all will be well this day.*

Romans 15:33

The God of peace be with you all.

81. Call upon my name

Come and take part in my goodness that I offer all of my children who call upon my name. As you go about your day, remember to think about me. Simply say hello and let me know what is on your mind. I wait patiently for you because I love you. I know the days can get very busy and it is easy to get distracted and forget about my presence. Some days are easier to walk with me than others. Some days you are so busy that you forget I am there to help lighten your load. Simply **call upon my name** and I am there for you. Some days there are great challenges and struggles where all you can do is cry out to me for help. That is what I am here for, to help you and to guide you. Whatever your day may hold, make a conscious effort to talk to me. A simple "Jesus!" is all it takes and I am there. I stand waiting for you to call on me. Let us walk through this day together and it will be well with your soul.

I will call upon your name

I will come and take part in your goodness that you offer all of your children who call upon your name. As I go about *my day, I will remember to think about you. I will simply say hello and let you know what is on my mind. You will wait patiently for me because you love me. You know the days can get very busy and it is easy to get distracted and forget about your presence. Some days are easier to walk with you than others. Some days I am so busy that I forget you are there to help lighten my load. **I will call upon your name** and you are there for me. Some days there are great challenges and struggles where all I can do is cry out to you for help. That is what you are here for, to help me and to guide me. Whatever my day may hold, I will make a conscious effort to talk to you. A simple "Jesus!" is all it takes and you are there. You stand waiting for me to call on you. I will let us walk through this day together and it will be well with my soul.*

Acts 2:21
And everyone who calls on the name
of the Lord will be saved.

82. Jesus, I receive your love

Your Word resonates deep within me. Your love flows over me like a never ending waterfall. Your Spirit within me makes your Word spring to life. I call on you and you answer me. I cry out to you and you hear my cry. You open the gates of heaven and come running to me with arms wide open. Jesus, I receive your love.

2 Peter 1:17
He received honor and glory from God the Father when the voice came to him from the Majestic Glory, saying, "This is my Son, whom I love; with him I am well pleased."

83. Come and follow me

Today is a brand new day to call on me and invite me to walk and talk with you. You can talk with me about anything and everything. Nothing is insignificant to me. As you talk to me and share your heart, my Spirit will speak to your spirit. I will shine a light into areas of darkness. I will bring you new insight and give you a different way of looking at the same situation. My Spirit within you will be your guide and I will bring you to higher grounds where you will have a broader view and greater perspective of the truth in your circumstances. **Come and follow me.** I will make a way for you where there seems to be no way. With me, all things are possible. I am with you as your helper. Lean on me when you are feeling weak and I will be your strength.

I will come and follow you

Today is a brand new day to call on you and invite you to walk and talk with me. I can talk with you about anything and everything. Nothing is insignificant to you. As I talk to you and share my heart, your Spirit will speak to my spirit. You will shine a light into areas of darkness. You will bring *me new insight and give me a different way of looking at the same situation. Your Spirit within me will be my guide and you will bring me to higher grounds where I will have a broader view and greater perspective of the truth in my circumstances. **I will come and follow you.** You will make a way for me where there seems to be no way. With you, all things are possible. You are with me as my helper. I will lean on you when I am feeling weak and you will be my strength.*

Matthew 16:24
Then Jesus said to his disciples, "Whoever wants to be my disciple must deny themselves and take up their cross and follow me.

84. Sing praises to your King of Kings (written for a music pastor)

Lift up your hands and heart to me! **Sing praises to your King of Kings** and Lord of Lords! Let my Spirit flow through your lips in song. My presence will come to rest upon you as you lift up my Name. The choirs of angels join you in song as they subdue the atmosphere among my people to bring in the Holy of Holies to be with you during your time of worship and praise. From on high the angels sound the trumpet and lead a processional making way for me to walk among you in the sanctuary. As my Spirit enters in, the darkness slips away and my light brings new insight and revelation into the hearts of my children. Lead the way for me, my child. All honor goes to the Father who sits with me upon His throne as you exalt my Name. My precious children are crying out to me, longing to hear a word that ministers to their hearts. Let my words flow freely through your lips as you share my heart with those all around you. I will give you a word in season for my children, a word that refreshes their souls and magnifies my presence within their hearts. As you make a way for me, so do I make a way for you. As you exalt me, so do I exalt you and lift you higher

217

and higher. Enter into my throne room with awe and wonder. I will set a crown of new life upon your head and all will see that I call you, my beloved one, my child who reverences my name with a pure heart. Your genuine worship is a light unto my people. Press into me in song and you will reap a harvest of righteousness and truth that will break the chains that bind and set my captive ones free.

I will sing praises to my King of Kings

I will lift up my hands and heart to you! ***I will sing praises to my King of Kings*** *and Lord of Lords! I will let your Spirit flow through my lips in song. Your presence will come to rest upon me as I lift up your Name. The choirs of angels join me in song as they subdue the atmosphere among your people to bring in the Holy of Holies to be with me during my time of worship and praise. From on high the angels sound the trumpet and lead a processional making way for you to walk among us in the sanctuary. As your Spirit enters in, the darkness slips away and your light brings new insight and revelation into the hearts of your children. I will lead the way for you, my Jesus. All honor goes to the Father who sits with you upon His throne as I exalt your Name. Your precious* *children are crying out to you, longing to hear a word that ministers to their hearts. I will let your words flow freely through my lips as I share your heart with those all around me. You will give me a word in season for your children, a word that refreshes their souls and magnifies your presence within their hearts. As I make a way for you, so do you make a way for me. As I exalt you, so do you exalt me and lift me higher and higher. I will enter into your throne room with awe and wonder. You will set a crown of new life upon my head and all will see that you call me, your beloved one, your child who reverences your name with a pure heart. My genuine worship is a light unto your people. I will press into you in song and I will reap a harvest of righteousness and truth that will break the chains that bind and set your captive ones free.*

Psalm 104:33
I will sing to the Lord all my life; I will sing praise to my God as long as I live.

85. I hear you

Your hope in me is like a song that fills a heart with gladness. Your thankfulness for all I do in your life brings joy to my heart. I desire the very best for you in all things, in everything that you do. I will reveal myself to you as you press into me. Do you know that I am your biggest advocate? I am the one who stands by your side at all times. When you are walking through a storm in life, just whisper my name. **I hear you** and am responding to your call. My Spirit will lead you in the way you should go as you keep your eyes focused on me. Take a moment to remember all the times that I have been with you and helped you through. This will strengthen your faith and be an encouragement to you. Stand up and be proud. The heavens are cheering you on. You have come so far along on your journey with me. You have been growing and learning in leaps and bounds along the way. Keep pressing forward. I admire you and am proud to call you, friend.

You hear me

*My hope in you is like a song that fills a heart with gladness. My thankfulness for all you do in my life brings joy to your heart. You desire the very best for me in all things, in everything that I do. You will reveal yourself to me as I press into you. I know that you are my biggest advocate. You are the one who stands by my side at all times. When I am walking through a storm in life, I will just whisper your name. **You hear me** and are responding to my call. Your Spirit will lead me in the way I should go as I keep my eyes focused on you. I will take a moment to remember all the times that you have been with me and helped me through. This will strengthen my faith and be an encouragement to me. I will stand up and be proud. The heavens are cheering me on. I have come so far along on my journey with you. I have been growing and learning in leaps and bounds along the way. I will keep pressing forward. You admire me and are proud to call me, friend.*

Psalm 4:3
Know that the Lord has set apart his faithful servant for himself; the Lord hears when I call to him.

86. I have called you to be a light

Beloved one, allow my rivers of living waters to cleanse you and remove anything that gets in the way of our communion with each other. There is an anointing upon your life. **I have called you to be a light** unto my children, to lead the lost and broken out of captivity. Allow my love to flow freely through you to others. I am increasing your compassion for my children and giving you a greater understanding of what it means to set the captives free. Surrender your heart to me and I will cut the cords that have kept you bound and limited you from fully stepping into the ministry I have called you to. As you are set free, so shall my light within you set others free.

You have called me to be a light

*Beloved Jesus, I will allow your rivers of living waters to cleanse me and remove anything that gets in the way of our communion with each other. There is an anointing upon my life. **You have called me to be a light** unto your children, to lead the lost and broken out of captivity. I will allow your love to flow freely through me to others. You are increasing* *my compassion for your children and giving me a greater understanding of what it means to set the captives free. I will surrender my heart to you and you will cut the cords that have kept me bound and limited me from fully stepping into the ministry you have called me to. As I am set free, so shall your light within me set others free.*

Isaiah 42:6
I, the Lord, have called you in righteousness; I will take hold of your hand. I will keep you and will make you to be a covenant for the people and a light for the Gentiles

87. My Word is food for your soul

Oh sweet and tender child, how I long for you to sit at my feet and nourish your soul with my Word of life which is everlasting and true. As you commit your time to me you are sowing seeds of faith and will reap a harvest of righteousness. Be at peace and rest in me. My hand of grace is upon you. Your feet are planted firmly on my Rock as you apply my Word to your daily life and walk in its truth. **My Word is food for your soul**. Step forth into this new day and walk with me. I am with you.

Your Word is food for my soul

*Oh sweet and tender Father, how you long for me to sit at your feet and nourish my soul with your Word of life which is everlasting and true. As I commit my time to you I am sowing seeds of faith and will reap a harvest of righteousness. I will be at peace and rest in you. Your hand of grace is upon me. My feet are planted firmly on your Rock as I apply your Word to my daily life and walk in its truth. **Your Word is food for my soul**. I will step forth into this new day and walk with you. You are with me.*

Hebrews 4:12

For the word of God is alive and active. Sharper than any double-edged sword, it penetrates even to dividing soul and spirit, joints and marrow; it judges the thoughts and attitudes of the heart.

88. Let me wipe the tears

I can see the sadness in your eyes and feel the sorrow in your heart. Do you know how much I love you, precious child? **Let me wipe the tears** that are streaming down your cheeks. Allow me to embrace you with my loving presence which is all about you now. I am here to bring you comfort. I am here to turn your thoughts that bring you sadness into thoughts that bring you joy. Allow me to take this pain you are feeling deep inside and gently wash it away with my love. I will fill the emptiness you are experiencing within with the fullness of my love. Lift up your head so that I may see your face, so that I may look into your eyes and tell you that I love you and that all will be well. Your sorrows will turn to joy as you see my hand of grace upon you. My mercies are new every morning and each day brings new light. Rest in me as you release it all into my hands. I am right by your side and I will never let you go.

I will let you wipe the tears

You can see the sadness in my eyes and feel the sorrow in my heart. Do I know how much you love me, Father? ***I will*** *let you wipe the tears that are streaming down my cheeks. I will allow you to embrace me with your loving presence which is all about me now. You are here to bring me comfort. You are here to turn my thoughts that bring me sadness into thoughts that bring me joy. I will allow you to take this pain I am feeling deep inside and gently wash it away with your love. You will fill the emptiness I am experiencing within with the fullness of your love. I will lift up my head so that you may see my face, so that you may look into my eyes and tell me that you love me and that all will be well. My sorrows will turn to joy as I see your hand of grace upon me. Your mercies are new every morning and each day brings new light. I will rest in you as I release it all into your hands. You are right by my side and you will never let me go.*

Lamentations 3:21-23
Yet this I call to mind and therefore I have hope:
Because of the Lord's great love we are not consumed,
for his compassions never fail. They are new every
morning; great is your faithfulness.

89. No matter what the enemy brings your way, you will not be defeated

Walking in my light will bring you peace that strengthens your spirit. During the storms of life, come and walk with me. I will cover you with a spiritual umbrella that keeps you protected from the schemes of the enemy who would like nothing more than to knock you off the Rock and keep you from getting up. What frustrates the enemy the most is that my children who are planted firmly on the Rock cannot be moved. **No matter what the enemy brings your way, you will not be defeated.** You may stumble, you may even fall at times, but my redemption goes before you and my strength in you gives you the power to overcome and rise back up again. So take my hand and rise up with me. Walk with me to the mountaintop and I will open your eyes to see things like you have never seen them before, through my eyes. The rains will dry up. The dark clouds will drift away. My sun will shine upon your life and you will experience the calm that always comes after the storm. When you look beneath your feet, there you will see the Rock. You will see that I have been there with you all along.

No matter what the enemy brings my way, I will not be defeated

*Walking in your light will bring me peace that strengthens my spirit. During the storms of life, I will come and walk with you. You will cover me with a spiritual umbrella that keeps me protected from the schemes of the enemy who would like nothing more than to knock me off the Rock and keep me from getting up. What frustrates the enemy the most is that your children who are planted firmly on the Rock cannot be moved. **No matter what the enemy brings my way, I will not be defeated**. I may stumble, I may even fall at times, but your redemption goes before me and your strength in me gives me the power to overcome and rise back up again. So I will take your hand and rise up with you. I will walk with you to the mountaintop and you will open my eyes to see things like I have never seen them before, through your eyes. The rains will dry up. The dark clouds will drift away. Your sun will shine upon my life and I will experience the calm that always comes after the storm. When I look beneath your feet, there I will see the Rock. I will see that you have been there with me all along.*

Psalm 91:11-12

For he will command his angels concerning you to guard you in all your ways; they will lift you up in their hands, so that you will not strike your foot against a stone.

90. I have great compassion for you

When you find yourself lost and abandoned by others, do not fear. Do not be sad for my mercies are new every morning and **I have great compassion for you**. I see the hurt in your eyes and can feel the hurt in your heart. You can be confident that I will always come to your rescue, no matter what you are going through. This may be a difficult day for you. Call out to me. I have much to share with you that will help you to be successful on your journey. Even when the path before you is filled with thorns and you do not know how to proceed, I will make the way for you. You do not have to figure everything out this moment. My wisdom will pour over you as you are ready to receive the truth of my Word. Do not be sad, my child. I love you so.

You have great compassion for me

*When I find myself lost and abandoned by others, I will not fear. I will not be sad for your mercies are new every morning and **you have great compassion for me**. You see the hurt in my eyes and can feel the hurt in my heart. I can be confident that you will always come to my rescue, no matter* *what I am going through. This may be a difficult day for me. I will call out to you. You have much to share with me that will help me to be successful on my journey. Even when the path before me is filled with thorns and I do not know how to proceed, you will make the way for me. I do not have to figure everything out this moment. Your wisdom will pour over me as I am ready to receive the truth of your Word. I will not be sad, my Jesus. You love me so.*

Exodus 22:27

When they cry out to me, I will hear,

for I am compassionate.

91. Delight yourself in me

Delight yourself in me and I will give you the desires of your heart. As you direct your thoughts toward me, I will pour out upon you riches from heaven. As you are led by my Spirit within you, I will give you all you need exactly how you need it. What I do as your Shepherd is lead you in the way you should go. You may feel at times as though I have not answered your prayers or that I am delayed in doing so. Be assured this day that I have heard all the cries of your heart. I have known every longing of your heart before you were even born. Imagine that. So when you come to me with requests, longings and desires it is of no surprise to me. When it seems as though I am delayed in answering, it is not because I have not heard you. My desire is that you have the very best. My answers often seem delayed, but as you seek after me and come to know me better you will realize that I am teaching you along the way how to trust in me. Remember, as I speak of in my Word, that hope does not disappoint. As you put your trust in me, hope is alive and breathing new life within you. As you mature in your faith and continue to develop and grow your relationship with me, you will find that delighting in me also means trusting in me. As you trust in me, you are laying yourself down and submitting to my perfect will. I am perfecting the desires of your heart to be in perfect alignment with my will. When your desire is in accord with my will and you have been made wholly ready to receive, it is then that you will begin to see your desires manifest in your life before your very eyes. I am faithful to my Word and all of my promises are true and everlasting. Delight yourself in me and I will give you the desires of your heart.

I will delight myself in you

I will delight myself in you and you will give me the desires of my heart. As I direct my thoughts toward you, you will pour out upon me riches from heaven. As I am led by your Spirit within me, you will give me all I need exactly how I need it. What you do as my Shepherd is lead me in the way I should go. I may feel at times as though you have not answered my prayers or that you are delayed in doing so. I will be assured this day that you have heard all the cries of my heart. You have known every longing of my heart before I was even born. I will imagine that. So when I come to you with requests, longings and desires it is of no surprise to you. When it seems as though you are delayed in answering, it is not because you have not heard me. Your desire is that I have the very best. Your answers often seem delayed, but as I seek after you and come to know you better I will realize that you are teaching me along the way how to trust in you. I will remember as you speak of in your Word that hope does not disappoint. As I put my trust in you, hope is alive and breathing new life within me. As I mature in my faith and continue to develop and grow my relationship with you, I will find that delighting in you also means trusting in you. As I trust in you, I am laying myself down and submitting to your perfect will. You are perfecting the desires of my heart to be in perfect alignment with your Will. When my desire is in accord with your will and I have been made wholly ready to receive, it is then that I will begin to see my desires manifest in my life before my very eyes. You are faithful to your Word and all of your promises are true and everlasting. I will delight myself in you and you will give me the desires of my heart.

Psalm 37:4 (NKJV)
Delight yourself also in the Lord, and He shall give you the desires of your heart.

92. There is no greater sacrifice

There is no greater sacrifice than to lay down your life for the sake of another. Laying down your life for another is putting aside your self-centered desires, attitudes, and beliefs for the sake of lifting another above yourself for the good of their soul.

There is no greater sacrifice

There is no greater sacrifice than to lay down my life for the sake of another. Laying down my life for another is putting aside my self-centered desires, attitudes, and beliefs for the sake of lifting another above myself for the good of their soul.

John 15:13

Greater love has no one than this: to lay down one's life for one's friends.

93. Go forth today and give!

I am teaching you how to be a giver. When you give, you also receive. Giving with faith in your God reaps the gift of receiving on a whole new level. This type of giving has no limits on how much you receive in return. When I am part of the equation, the receiving now becomes a great mystery of grace, the grace I bestow upon you out of a love that is fathomless. This type of giving brings exuberant joy to my heart which loves you beyond compare. **Go forth today and give** to others with faith in your Savior, the Giver of all Givers, and I will bless you in what you receive in countless measure!

I will go forth today and give

You are teaching me how to be a giver. When I give, I also receive. Giving with faith in my God reaps the gift of receiving on a whole new level. This type of giving has no limits on how much I receive in return. When you are part of the equation, the receiving now becomes a great mystery of grace, the grace you bestow upon me out of a love that is fathomless. This type of giving brings exuberant joy to your

heart which loves me beyond compare. *I will go forth today
and give to others with faith in my Savior, the Giver of all
Givers, and you will bless me in what I receive in countless measure!*

Acts 20:35

*In everything I did, I showed you that by this kind of hard
work we must help the weak, remembering the words
the Lord Jesus himself said: It is more blessed
to give than to receive.*

94. I will be with you always

Look deep within your heart and there will you find me. I sit waiting to talk with you from the throne room I established in your heart when you asked me to become the Lord of your life. You may remember the very moment you first took a leap of faith and called upon my name, your Jesus. Perhaps you have always held me in your heart but have come to know me in different ways through time and seasons, joys and sorrows. It is not how you came to know me and when I became real to you that matters the most. What truly matters is that you do know me and believe in me. I suffered on the cross to redeem you so that you could live life eternally. **I will be with you always**.

You will be with me always

I will look deep within my heart and there I will find you. You sit waiting to talk with me from the throne room you established in my heart when I asked me to become the Lord of my life. I may remember the very moment I first took a leap of faith and called upon your name, my Jesus. Perhaps I have always held you in my heart but have come to know you in different ways through time and seasons, joys and sorrows. It is not how I came to know you and when you became real to me that matters the most. What truly matters is that I do know you and believe in you. You suffered on the cross to redeem me so that I could live life eternally. **You will be with me always.**

2 Chronicles 15:2

The Lord is with you when you are with him.

95. My glory is upon you!

Surrounding you are my guardian angels that I have appointed to watch over you. As you rest tonight I will go before you and orchestrate the rising of the sun to greet you in the morning hours. There is a beautifully choreographed symphony of love flowing down upon you from the heavens. Cascades of pure and living waters are cleansing your heart and mind as your thoughts float into dreams. The fragrance of my presence envelops your calm and tender spirit. Your humility shines like a radiant moonbeam lighting up the starry night skies. The song I am singing over you will fill your heart with gladness and bring strength to your soul. A new and glorious day is arising. Make way for the King of Kings! The trumpets sound and the angels sing. Behold! I am entering your heart this day for you to rise up as my ambassador to share my goodness with all those I place along your path. Be of good cheer for you will radiate my light and all will see the magnificence of my love as you greet my children with a smile. **My glory is upon you!**

You glory is upon me!

*Surrounding me are your guardian angels that you have appointed to watch over me. As I rest tonight you will go before me and orchestrate the rising of the sun to greet me in the morning hours. There is a beautifully choreographed symphony of love flowing down upon me from the heavens. Cascades of pure and living waters are cleansing my heart and mind as my thoughts float into dreams. The fragrance of your presence envelops my calm and tender spirit. My humility shines like a radiant moonbeam lighting up the starry night skies. The song you are singing over me will fill my heart with gladness and bring strength to my soul. A new and glorious day is arising. I will make way for the King of Kings! The trumpets sound and the angels sing. I will behold! You are entering my heart this day for me to rise up as your ambassador to share your goodness with all those you place along my path. I will be of good cheer for I will radiate your light and all will see the magnificence of your love as I greet your children with a smile. **Your glory is upon me!***

Psalm 3:3
But you, Lord, are a shield around me, my glory, the One who lifts my head high.

96. I am raising up a standard against the enemy

I am with you this day to edify you and lift you up. Come along and soar to new heights with me. **I am raising up a standard against the enemy.** Stand firm and push back against the darkness and break through with my light. This battle you are in, whether it be small or seemingly insurmountable, you are not in it alone. You are never alone. You have the very Creator of the Universe standing by your side cheering you on to victory. Never underestimate the power of my love. All you need to do is trust in me. Trust that my Word is true and everlasting. What I promised to my children in days of old are promises I made for you too knowing the very time, very moment, very minute you would exist. You are here for a purpose. I loved you into existence. It is true that you were created by my very hand out of love. And you, just the way you are, imperfections and all, are my priceless masterpiece. There is hidden treasure in you that is yet to be discovered. Just wait until you find what I have stored up for you in the treasuries of your heart. You will be utterly amazed. You are amazing to me. Just as a parent smiles in adoration of their child, so do I beam with adoration over you.

You are raising up a standard against the enemy

You are with me this day to edify me and lift me up. You will come along and soar to new heights with me. **You are raising up a standard against the enemy.** *I will stand firm and push back against the darkness and break through with your light. This battle I am in, whether it be small or seemingly insurmountable, I am not in it alone. I am never alone. I have the very Creator of the Universe standing by my side cheering me on to victory. I will never underestimate the power of your love. All I need to do is trust in you. I will trust that your Word is true and everlasting. What you promised to your children in days of old are promises you made for me too knowing the very time, very moment, very minute I would exist. I am here for a purpose. You love me into existence. It is true that I was created by your very hand out of love. And I, just the way I am, imperfections and all, am your priceless masterpiece. There is hidden treasure in me that is yet to be discovered. I will just wait until I find what you have stored up for me in the treasuries of my heart.*

I will be utterly amazed. I am amazing to you. Just as a parent smiles in adoration of their child, so do you beam with adoration over me.

Isaiah 59:19

So shall they fear the name of the Lord from the west, And His glory from the rising of the sun; When the enemy comes in like a flood, The Spirit of the Lord will lift up a standard against him.

97. Jesus, you are the joy of my heart

Oh joy! My heart leaps within me at the sound of your name ~ Jesus. All that is within me yearns to know you and to love you. **Jesus, you are the joy of my heart!** *Your spirit is alive within me. No matter what I am going through, you are the one that always pulls me through. I know you have never forsaken me, even in my darkest hours. You, my Jesus, are the song of my heart. Though a day may pull me in a thousand different directions, your love for me is constant. Your love is the calm of my heart. My soul rests in you and I am secure.*

Psalm 28:7
The Lord is my strength and my shield; my heart trusts in him, and he helps me. My heart leaps for joy, and with my song I praise him.

98. I have you in the palm of my hand

You are my lovely, radiant flower, full of brilliant colors. My love surrounds your heart and very being. Even though you have internal struggles where your mind can rage in war with itself, I am the calming voice that brings you into the light and out of the darkness. Your wisdom is growing as you seek to overcome areas in your life that have kept you locked into those cold, dark places. It only takes a tiny flame to bring light to a room. That is the flame you need to follow after, the light of my Holy Spirit, the fire of my righteousness and power. If all you can see is a tiny flicker of light, that is all the hope you need to hold onto for the day, for my light will see you through and you will make it out of the dark place. Your struggles here are nothing in comparison to the glory that you will behold when I return. All of your efforts in putting your trust in me are not in vain. They define you. Your unwavering faithfulness brings adoration to my heart for you. I look upon you with great admiration and compassion. Not one tear shed goes unnoticed by me. And those times when you are so in pain that you don't even have the energy to shed a tear, I know what you are feeling and going through. **I have you in the palm of my hand**. You are more than a survivor, you are a conqueror! Great is the hand of the Almighty upon your life. Greatness shall go before you and follow you wherever you go. Glorious child, I love you so. Take my hand and walk with me. I have something special to show you this day.

You have me in the palm of your hand

I am your lovely, radiant flower, full of brilliant colors. Your love surrounds my heart and very being. Even though I have internal struggles where my mind can rage in war with itself, you are the calming voice that brings me into the light and out of the darkness. My wisdom is growing as I seek to overcome areas in my life that have kept me locked into those cold, dark places. It only takes a tiny flame to bring light to a room. That is the flame I need to follow after, the light of your Holy Spirit, the fire of your righteousness and power. If all I can see is a tiny flicker of light, that is all the hope I need to hold onto for the day, for your light will see me through and I will make it out of the dark place. My struggles here are nothing in comparison to the glory that I will behold when you return. All of my efforts in putting my trust in you are not in vain. They define me. My unwavering faithfulness brings adoration to your heart for me. You look upon me with great admiration and compassion. Not one tear shed goes unnoticed by you. And those times when I am so in pain that I don't even have the energy to shed a tear, you know what I am feeling and going through. **You have me in the palm of your hand.** *I am more than a survivor, I am a conqueror! Great is the hand of the Almighty upon my life. Greatness shall go before me and follow me wherever I go. Glorious Jesus, I love you so. I will take your hand and walk with you. You have something special to show me this day.*

Isaiah 49:16
See, I have engraved you on the palms of my hands; your walls are ever before me.

99. I have overcome

My beloved child, seek not after the things of this world. Seek after the gifts of the Spirit and treasures of the heart that are everlasting and true. Mighty is your Maker and wonderfully have you been made. Oh, the many trials you have been through! You have been forged in the fire for a purpose far greater than you can imagine. You have sought after me and my reward, one of my rewards, is eternal and life giving wisdom. Take this gift and share it with those who are walking the same walk. Share this gift to the lost and broken hearted that have gone through many fiery trials. This is your testimony and the hope you give to others. **I have overcome** so that you may overcome. You have overcome so that others may overcome. Rest assured that it has been worth the fight. Be thankful for your trials for they shall bring you great strength in the days to come.

You have overcome

My Jesus, I will not seek after the things of this world. I will seek after the gifts of the Spirit and treasures of the heart that are everlasting and true. Mighty is my Maker and wonderfully have I been made. Oh, the many trials I have been through! I have been forged in the fire for a purpose far greater than I can imagine. I have sought after you and your reward, one of your rewards, is eternal and life giving wisdom. I will take this gift and share it with those who are walking the same walk. I will share this gift to the lost and broken that have gone through many fiery trials. This is my testimony and the hope I give to others. **You have overcome** *so that I may overcome. I have overcome so that others may overcome. I will rest assured that it has been worth the fight. I will be thankful for my trials for they shall bring me great strength in the days to come.*

John 16:33

"I have told you these things, so that in me you may have peace. In this world you will have trouble. But take heart! I have overcome the world."

100. I will rescue you

My goodness is flowing upon your life from the treasuries I have stored up for you in heaven. Each time that you call upon my name, trust in me. I will answer. I am coming. I am with you. Many of your years have been laden with sorrows and your cries have pierced my heart. I look upon you with great compassion and want you to believe that everything will work out. Not everything in this life of yours will go perfectly. This is a fallen world, but I have come to restore and redeem my beloved children. You are my beloved child and **I will rescue you**.

You will rescue me

Your goodness is flowing upon my life from the treasuries you have stored up for me in heaven. Each time that I call upon your name, I will trust in you. You will answer. You are coming. You are with me. Many of my years have been laden with sorrows and my cries have pierced your heart. You look upon me with great compassion and want me to believe that everything will work out. Not everything in this life of mine will go perfectly. This is a fallen world, but you have come to restore and redeem your beloved children. I am your beloved child and you will rescue me.

Psalm 18:19

He brought me out into a spacious place; he rescued me because he delighted in me.

101. Rest upon my shoulders

There are times when you may feel weary, worn out, burdened. There are times when you make poor choices. There are times when you feel like giving up or throwing in the towel. These are the times you especially need to press into me. Do not continue condemning yourself for things you have done wrong. You are forgiven, my child. Now, come, let us lay out a new path together. Consider us a team. I am here to coach you and to lead you into greater things. You may get tired along the way but I ask that you do not give up. Remember, it is darkest before the dawn. You never know what glory the next day may behold. **Rest upon my shoulders** and allow me to recharge your battery, to re-energize your spirit so you can continue upward on your journey. I will lighten your load and bring peace to you this day as you turn it all over to me.

I will rest upon your shoulders

There are times when I may feel weary, worn out, burdened. There are times when I make poor choices. There are times when I feel like giving up or throwing in the towel.

*These are the times I especially need to press into you. I will not continue condemning myself for things I have done wrong. I am forgiven, my Jesus. Now, I will come, I will let us lay out a new path together. I will consider us a team. You are here to coach me and to lead me into greater things. I may get tired along the way but you ask that I do not give up. I will remember, it is darkest before the dawn. I never know what glory the next day may behold. **I will rest upon your shoulders** and allow you to recharge my battery, to re-energize my spirit so I can continue upward on my journey. You will lighten my load and bring peace to me this day as I turn it all over to you.*

Matthew 11:28
Come to me, all you who are weary and burdened, and I will give you rest.

102. I gave my Son

The way into my heart is through loving and through prayer. When you pray, it is an act of faith. Your prayer is also an act of love. Come! Sit by my side and talk with me. Express your heart and deepest thoughts. I am listening. As you let down your walls and expose your vulnerabilities to me, I can begin to penetrate those dark and troublesome areas with my light. My light will bring healing. The deeper your prayer life is with me, the deeper our relationship grows. Moment by moment, layer by layer I will uncover anything that keeps you from being closer to me. I will reveal to you truths about yourself. Once the truth is unveiled, you will be able to see yourself from a new vantage point. You will begin to see yourself the way I see you. I want you to know how deep and wide is my love for you and that nothing can separate you from my love. My love for you flows like a river that will never dry up. Imagine trying to wrap your arms around the ocean. It would seem impossible to grasp something so great in your arms. But what you may not realize is that an entire ocean is but a tiny drop of water compared to the gift you now hold in your heart. **I gave my Son** so that he may live and reign in your heart forever. So remember, when you enter into prayer, you are talking to the King of all Kings and you have my undivided attention. Nothing is insignificant to me. If it matters to you, it matters to me for I take each and every one of your concerns to heart.

You gave your Son

The way into your heart is through loving and through prayer. When I pray, it is an act of faith. My prayer is also an act of love. I will come! I will sit by your side and talk with you. I will express my heart and deepest thoughts. You are listening. As I let down my walls and expose my vulnerabilities to you, you can begin to penetrate those dark and troublesome areas with your light. Your light will bring healing. The deeper my prayer life is with you, the deeper our relationship grows. Moment by moment, layer by layer you will uncover anything that keeps me from being closer to you. You will reveal to me truths about myself. Once the truth is unveiled, I will be able to see myself from a new vantage point. I will begin to see myself the way you see me. You want me to know how deep and wide is your love for me and that nothing can separate me from your love. Your love for me flows like a river that will never dry up. I will *imagine trying to wrap my arms around the ocean. It would seem impossible to grasp something so great in my arms. But what I may not realize is that an entire ocean is but a tiny drop of water compared to the gift I now hold in my heart. **You gave your Son** so that he may live and reign in my heart forever. So I will remember, when I enter into prayer, I am talking to the King of all Kings and I have your undivided attention. Nothing is insignificant to you. If it matters to me, it matters to you for you take each and every one of my concerns to heart.*

John 3:16

For God so loved the world that he gave his one and only Son, that whoever believes in him shall not perish but have eternal life.

103. I am calling you higher and higher

My beloved child, as you seek my face I will in turn open the heavens unto you giving you access to the glorious mysteries of my Kingdom. As your heart and mind are enlightened, your understanding of my Word will increase exponentially. This will open doors in your life that you never realized were even there. My light will shine upon the path before you and you will see things like you have never seen them before. You will be able to take your new found wisdom and apply it to your daily life. This will enable you to overcome obstacles that have impeded your growth and forward momentum. You will wake up singing new and glorious praises unto your Father who has brought you new light to brighten your day. You will receive a greater awareness of who you are in my eyes and all that I have called you to be. **I am calling you higher and higher**. Go forth and bring my light into the world this day.

You are calling me higher and higher

My beloved Jesus, as I seek your face you will in turn open the heavens unto me giving me access to the glorious mysteries of your Kingdom. As my heart and mind are enlightened, my understanding of your Word will increase exponentially. This will open doors in my life that I never realized were even there. Your light will shine upon the path before me and I will see things like I have never seen them before. I will be able to take my new found wisdom and apply it to my daily life. This will enable me to overcome obstacles that have impeded my growth and forward momentum. I will wake up singing new and glorious praises unto my Father who has brought me new light to brighten my day. I will receive a greater awareness of who I am in your eyes and all that you have called me to be. **You are calling me higher and higher**. I will go forth and bring your light into the world this day.

2 Corinthians 3:18
But we all, with unveiled face, beholding as in a mirror the glory of the Lord, are being transformed into the same image from glory to glory, just as by the Spirit of the Lord.

104. I eagerly anticipate the moments we share together

Never has there been a time or place where I have not existed, for I am in all things, with all things and have given all things. In days to come, the light of my love will overpower the lost and the broken in ways that have never been known to man. For I am a God that loves beyond compare and I would have it that all of my children draw near me so that I can empower them to live righteously and to walk with blessing and goodness surrounding them. I want for you to know that I am a merciful God, and even if you feel as though you are not where you would like to be in relationship with me, know that it is never too late. Today is the day to begin and remember that every day as you awake is a new day. **I eagerly anticipate the moments we share together**. I love the daily conversations we have with each other. The more time you spend developing a relationship with me, the closer we will become. As with everything, the more you put into it, the more you get out of it. Love me with all of your heart, mind, strength and soul and in doing so I will teach you how to love others the way they deserve to be loved. I love all my children and there is not one soul that is not precious in my eyes. My heart is saddened when my children deny my name and walk through their lives as if they do not need me. I daily give my children the opportunity to rely on me, to trust in me, to walk with me. As you walk with me, so do I walk with you. Even when you do not feel my presence, know that I am always by your side. Never once have I forsaken those who belong to me. In times to come, as you call upon my name, you will see a change in the atmosphere around you, a change in the attitudes of my children as I give them new understanding of my undying love for them. Today as you call upon my name, know that you are loved. I give my children what they need. Give your very best to me and I will always give my very best to you.

You eagerly anticipate the moments we share together

Never has there been a time or place where you have not existed, for you are in all things, with all things and have given all things. In days to come, the light of your love will overpower the lost and the broken in ways that have never been known to man. For you are a God that loves beyond compare and you would have it that all of your children draw near you so that you can empower them to live righteously and to walk with blessing and goodness surrounding them. You want for me to know that you are a merciful God, and even if I feel as though I am not where I would like to be in relationship with you, I will know that it is never too late. Today is the day to begin and remember that every day as I awake is a new day. **You eagerly anticipate the moments we share together.** *You love the daily conversations we have with each other. The more time I spend developing a relationship with you, the closer we will become. As with everything, the more I put into it, the more I get out of it. I will love you with all of my heart, mind, and soul and in doing so you will teach me how to love others the way they deserve to be loved. You love all your children and there is not one soul that is not precious in your eyes. Your heart is saddened when your children deny your name and walk through their lives as if they do not need you. You daily give your children the opportunity to rely on you, to trust in you, to walk with you. As I walk with you, so do you walk with me. Even when I do not feel your presence, I know that you are always by my side. Never once have you forsaken those who belong to you. In times to come, as I call upon your name, I will see a change in the atmosphere around me, a* *change in the attitudes of your children as you give them new understanding of your undying love for them. Today as I call upon your name, I will know that I am loved. You give your children what they need. I will give my very best to you and you will always give your very best to me.*

Psalm 42:1

As the deer pants for streams of water,
so my soul pants for you, my God.

105. **I am true to my Word always**

My heart goes out to you this day. Whenever you feel afraid, run to me and I will shelter you in my arms. Do not fear for I am with you always. I watch over you with loving kindness. Sometimes you are overcome with thoughts that seem to set your mind in a tail spin. During these times focus not on the issues that pervade your thoughts. Instead, release those thoughts into my hands. Focus not on your concerns. Focus on me. Ponder on the greatness and majesty of your God, your Almighty Father. **I am true to my Word always**. You may feel at times that I have not followed through on my promises. I have. There is a time and season for all things. When it is the right time, my perfect time, you will see my light. I will reveal to you my purpose and perfect will. Do not lose heart. Keep your eyes fixed on me and in time you will receive your reward. My blessings and peace are ever before you. Just continue to press in and keep your eyes and heart focused on me and my presence. Rest in me today and it will be well with your soul.

You are true to your Word always

Your heart goes out to me this day. Whenever I feel afraid, I will run to you and you will shelter me in your arms. I will not fear for you are with me always. You watch over me with loving kindness. Sometimes I am overcome with thoughts that seem to set my mind in a tail spin. During these times I will not focus on the issues that pervade my thoughts. Instead, I will release those thoughts into your hands. I will not focus on my concerns. I will focus on you. I will ponder on the greatness and majesty of my God, my Almighty Father. **You are true to your Word always.** *I may feel at times that you have not followed through on your promises. You have. There is a time and season for all things. When it is the right time, your perfect time, I will see your light. You will reveal to me your purpose and perfect will. I will not lose heart. I will keep my eyes fixed on you and in time I will receive my reward. Your blessings and peace are ever before me. I will continue to press in and keep my eyes and heart focused on you and your presence. I will rest in you today and it will be well with my soul.*

Psalm 33:4
For the word of the Lord is right and true; he is faithful in all he does.

106. I will shower you with my loving kindness

Today as you look to me, **I will shower you with my loving kindness**. Even when your heart is troubled, know that I am with you. When you are searching for answers deep within your heart, know that you are going to find those answers as you direct your thoughts toward me. Trying to figure all the details out on your own will only cause anxiety. I would have it that you turn toward me. I would have it that you experience peace. I am the master architect of your life and I am building something great and new within you this season. Be refreshed this day and rest assured that I love you and am working on your behalf, in all circumstances. Turn your face toward me, my beloved, so that I may give you a smile that melts your heart. I am smiling upon you this day.

You will shower me with your loving kindness

*Today as I look to you, **you will shower me with your loving kindness**. Even when my heart is troubled, I will know that you are with me. When I am searching for answers deep within my heart, I will know that I am going to find those* *answers as I direct my thoughts toward you. Trying to figure all the details out on my own will only cause anxiety. You would have it that I turn toward you. You would have it that I experience peace. You are the master architect of my life and you are building something great and new within me this season. I will be refreshed this day and rest assured that you love me and are working on my behalf, in all circumstances. I will turn my face toward you, my Jesus, so that you may give me a smile that melts my heart. You are smiling upon me this day.*

Jeremiah 31:3
I have loved you with an everlasting love; I have drawn you with unfailing kindness.

107. I will never leave you

Treasure of my heart, I love you. My love for you is deep and wide. It extends to the heavens and beyond. My love for you has no end. I have loved you always. You are never outside of my love. I know that at times it is difficult for you to receive my love. This happens when you are down on yourself and discouraged. I want you to open your heart to me at these times and let my love surround you. This will bring healing and restoration. My love for you lifts you up. It brings you to a place where you can be confident that I am with you. I know that you feel alone sometimes, and there are many who feel alone all the time. You are never alone. Why is it that you do not always feel my presence? Because it is in these time that I am refining you and calling you to deeper places. When you do not feel me, you come looking for me more fervently. And as you seek me, you shall find me. **I will never leave you.** You may feel like you are in the dark but I am the light within you that keeps you moving forward. I am your hope. Be encouraged in my love for you. I give it to you in great measure. Oh, that you could fathom my love for you! One day, you will. That day is on its way.

Be ready for it, for it will take many by surprise if they are not seeking after me. Treasure of my heart, I love you.

You will never leave me

*My Father, you love me. Your love for me is deep and wide. It extends to the heavens and beyond. Your love for me has no end. You have loved me always. I am never outside of your love. You know that at times it is difficult for me to receive your love. This happens when I am down on myself and discouraged. You want me to open my heart to you at these times and let your love surround me. This will bring healing and restoration. Your love for me lifts me up. It brings me to a place where I can be confident that you are with me. You know that I feel alone sometimes, and there are many who feel alone all the time. I am never alone. Why is it that I do not always feel your presence? Because it is in these time that you are refining me and calling me to deeper places. When I do not feel you, I come looking for you more fervently. And as I seek you, I shall find you. **You will never leave me**. I may feel like I am in the dark but you are the light within me that keeps me moving forward. You are my hope. I will be encouraged in your love for me. You give it to me* *in great measure. Oh, that I could fathom your love for me! One day, I will. That day is on its way. I will be ready for it, for it will take many by surprise if they are not seeking after you. My Father, I love you.*

Deuteronomy 31:8
The Lord himself goes before you and will be with you; he will never leave you nor forsake you. Do not be afraid; do not be discouraged."

108. The power of my Word

Beloved one, I have come so that you may find rest. The days of your life at times can be exhausting. I know this. I am here to refresh your spirit and give you the energy you need to make it through your busy days. In the midst of it all, remember to pause and look up to me. I will give you what you need to whether any storm that comes your way. Some days you will walk with confidence and surety in me. Other days because of the enemy's wicked ways, you may be bombarded with negative thoughts that bring you down. Be aware that these thoughts do not come from me. When this occurs, draw upon my Word and speak the truth over yourself. My Word will break through any wall that the enemy tries to surround you with. Do you know **the power of my Word**? It is life giving and will empower you to walk in my ways despite your circumstances. Be refreshed in me. I am your greatest advocate and I have your best interest at heart, at all times. My arms are wide open. Let me embrace you with my love this day. All will be well.

The power of your Word

*Beloved Jesus, you have come so that I may find rest. The days of my life at times can be exhausting. You know this. You are here to refresh my spirit and give me the energy I need to make it through my busy days. In the midst of it all, I will remember to pause and look up to you. You will give me what I need to whether any storm that comes my way. Some days I will walk with confidence and surety in you. Other days because of the enemy's wicked ways, I may be bombarded with negative thoughts that bring me down. I will be aware that these thoughts do not come from you. When this occurs, I will draw upon your Word and speak the truth over myself. Your Word will break through any wall that the enemy tries to surround me with. Do I know **the power of your Word**? It is life giving and will empower me to walk in your ways despite my circumstances. I will be refreshed in you. You are my greatest advocate and you have my best interest at heart, at all times. Your arms are wide open. I will let you embrace me with your love this day. All will be well.*

Psalm 33:6
By the word of the Lord the heavens were made, their
starry host by the breath of his mouth.

273

109. I am your Rock

You are a prized pearl in my Kingdom. You have walked down a path that very few have journeyed. You have been brave. Your journey to my heart has lifted you up to a new vantage point where you are now able to see far beyond what you ever thought you could see. I give you glimpses of my glory as you invite me in to dwell with you. These glimpses are the sparks of hope that I keep alive within your heart. Oh, your hope in victory is just the beginning. I have called you to be with me in a new way. When I move, there is nothing that can get in my way. There is a tidal wave of my love coming in the near future that will hit the land with force. Anyone that is in the way of this move of the Spirit will be impacted deep within their hearts, both believers in me and non-believers. It will be a day of reckoning. I will show you things in the realm of the Spirit that will lead you in the way you should go. Be not afraid, for I am doing a good thing in the land. There will be a fresh anointing on my chosen ones and I will impart to them many new gifts that will help them to call my children home. I want you to know that you are and always will be in the palm of my hand. You cannot be moved for **I am your Rock**. I am your firm foundation.

Cling to me and I will make a way for you in the desert. I will be your refreshing spring of life giving waters. Read my Word. Sing my Word. Listen to my Word. Are you ready? I am coming soon.

You are my Rock

I am a prized pearl in your Kingdom. I have walked down a path that very few have journeyed. I have been brave. My journey to your heart has lifted me up to a new vantage point where I am now able to see far beyond what I ever thought I could see. You give me glimpses of your glory as I invite you in to dwell with me. These glimpses are the sparks of hope that you keep alive within my heart. Oh, my hope in victory is just the beginning. You have called me to be with you in a new way. When you move, there is nothing that can get in your way. There is a tidal wave of your love coming in the near future that will hit the land with force. Anyone that is in the way of this move of the Spirit will be impacted deep within their hearts, both believers in you and non-believers. It will be a day of reckoning. You will show me things in the realm of the Spirit that will lead me in the way I should go. I will not be afraid, for you are doing a good thing in the land.

*There will be a fresh anointing on your chosen ones and you will impart to them many new gifts that will help them to call your children home. You want me to know that I am and always will be in the palm of your hand. I cannot be moved for **you are my Rock**. You are my firm foundation. I will cling to you and you will make a way for me in the desert. You will be my refreshing spring of life giving waters. I will read your Word. I will sing your Word. I will listen to your Word. Am I ready? You are coming soon.*

Deuteronomy 32:4
He is the Rock, his works are perfect, and all his ways are just. A faithful God who does no wrong, upright and just is he.

110. You will be victorious in me and through me

Oh sweet and beloved friend of mine, how I long to have you sit at my feet and listen to me. I have so much to share with you about yourself. What I have to share will bring you all the hope in the world that you need to make it through the day. When you feel like you have been abandoned, know that I am with you. I am nearer to you than you can even imagine. As you look up to me, so am I looking upon you with great admiration. I want you to know that despite the odds, **you will be victorious in me and through me**. Remember that I will always make a way for you where there seems to be no way. I am setting the course by which you can run across the finish line and win the prize I have been waiting to give all of my children who keep their heart and minds focused on me. I am the one that brings life and freedom. You are well on your way to victory. Stay the course, my friend. I am with you always.

I will be victorious in you and through you

Oh sweet and beloved Jesus of mine, how you long to have me sit at your feet and listen to you. You have so much to share with me about myself. *What you have to share will bring me all the hope in the world that I need to make it through the day. When I feel like I have been abandoned, I will know that you are with me. You are nearer to me than I can even imagine. As I look up to you, so are you looking upon me with great admiration. You want me to know that despite the odds,* **I will be victorious in you and through you.** *I will remember that you will always make a way for me where there seems to be no way. You are setting the course by which I can run across the finish line and win the prize you have been waiting to give all of your children who keep their heart and minds focused on you. You are the one that brings life and freedom. I am well on my way to victory. I will stay the course, my Jesus. You are with me always.*

Psalm 91:14-16

Because he loves me, says the Lord, I will rescue him; I will protect him, for he acknowledges my name. He will call on me, and I will answer him; I will be with him in trouble, I will deliver him and honor him. With long life I will satisfy him and show him my salvation.

111. *Thank you, Jesus*

Dear Lord, you are my rock and my fortress. Whenever I call upon your name, you are there. No matter what I am going through, I know that it will all work out because I put my trust in you. Thank you for standing by my side. Thank you for carrying me through. Thank you for the gift of faith that you placed in my heart so many years ago. I have been lost so many times in my life but you have been faithful to rescue me, to pull me out of the lion's den unharmed. Oh Lord, words cannot even begin to describe the greatness of your love for me and for all of your children. Draw me into your heart and never let me go. I am safe in your arms. Thank you for your Word and all of your loving promises. I put my trust in you because I know that you will never fail me. Your love carries me through it all. You have snatched me out of the enemy's hands so many times. How can I ever express my thankfulness to you? The words of hope you give me for others is my thank offering unto you. My heart goes out to you this day and your love rests upon me. Shine your light into the hearts of all your children so that they may come to know the goodness of your love. You are my greatest treasure and my truest love. **Thank you, Jesus.**

2 Corinthians 4:15

All this is for your benefit, so that the grace that is reaching more and more people may cause thanksgiving to overflow to the glory of God.

Revelation 11:17

We give thanks to you, Lord God Almighty, the One who is and who was, because you have taken your great power and have begun to reign.

2 Thessalonians 3:16

Now may the Lord of peace himself give you peace at all times and in every way. The Lord be with all of you.

Hebrews 11:1 (NLT)

Faith is the confidence that what we hope for will actually happen; it gives us assurance about things we cannot see.

D ana Howard lives in Washington State with her husband John and has three beautiful sons, Zachary, Jonathan, and Josiah – the son who was adopted by a wonderful family to whom she will forever be grateful.

CPSIA information can be obtained at www.ICGtesting.com
Printed in the USA
LVOW12s1825200813

348827LV00002B/307/P